Pipeline Accident Report

Rupture of Piney Point Oil Pipeline and Release of Fuel Oil Near Chalk Point, Maryland April 7, 2000

NTSB/PAR-02/01
PB2002-916501
Notation 7285A
Adopted July 23, 2002

National Transportation Safety Board
490 L'Enfant Plaza, S.W.
Washington, D.C. 20594

National Transportation Safety Board. 2002. *Rupture of Piney Point Oil Pipeline and Release of Fuel Oil Near Chalk Point, Maryland, April 7, 2000.* Pipeline Accident Report NTSB/PAR-02/01. Washington, DC.

Abstract: On the morning of April 7, 2000, the Piney Point Oil Pipeline system, which was owned by the Potomac Electric Power Company, experienced a pipe failure at the Chalk Point Generating Station in southeastern Prince George's County, Maryland. The release was not discovered and addressed by the contract operating company, Support Terminal Services, Inc., until the late afternoon. Approximately 140,400 gallons of fuel oil were released into the surrounding wetlands and Swanson Creek and, subsequently, the Patuxent River as a result of the accident. No injuries were caused by the accident, which cost approximately $71 million for environmental response and clean-up operations.

The safety issues discussed in this report are the sufficiency of the evaluation procedures for pipe wrinkles; the efficiency of the leak notification procedures; and the effectiveness of the incident command.

As a result of its investigation, the National Transportation Safety Board issued safety recommendations to the Research and Special Programs Administration and the Environmental Protection Agency.

Contents

Appendixes

Acronyms and Abbreviations

API -- American Petroleum Institute

CFR -- *Code of Federal Regulations*

EPA -- Environmental Protection Agency

Mirant -- Mirant Piney Point, LLP

Pepco -- Potomac Electric Power Company

RSPA -- Research and Special Programs Administration

SCADA -- supervisory control and data acquisition

ST Services -- Support Terminal Services, Inc.

Executive Summary

On the morning of April 7, 2000, the Piney Point Oil Pipeline system, which was owned by the Potomac Electric Power Company, experienced a pipe failure at the Chalk Point Generating Station in southeastern Prince George's County, Maryland. The release was not discovered and addressed by the contract operating company, Support Terminal Services, Inc., until the late afternoon. Approximately 140,400 gallons of fuel oil were released into the surrounding wetlands and Swanson Creek and, subsequently, the Patuxent River as a result of the accident. No injuries were caused by the accident, which cost approximately $71 million for environmental response and clean-up operations.

The National Transportation Safety Board determines that the probable cause of the April 7, 2000, Piney Point Oil Pipeline accident at the Potomac Electric Power Company's Chalk Point, Maryland, generating station was a fracture in a buckle in the pipe that was undiscovered because the data from an in-line inspection tool were interpreted inaccurately as representing a T-piece. Contributing to the magnitude of the fuel oil release were inadequate operating procedures and practices for monitoring the flow of fuel oil through the pipeline to ensure timely leak detection.

This report discusses the following major safety issues:

- The sufficiency of the evaluation procedures for pipe wrinkles;
- The efficiency of the leak notification procedures; and,
- The effectiveness of the incident command.

In addition to these issues, the Safety Board's investigation addressed the leak detection procedures used on the Piney Point Oil Pipeline and the analysis of the pipeline in-line inspection results.

As a result of its investigation of this accident, the Safety Board makes safety recommendations to the Research and Special Programs Administration and the Environmental Protection Agency.

Factual Information

Accident Synopsis

On the morning of April 7, 2000, the Piney Point Oil Pipeline system, which was owned by the Potomac Electric Power Company (Pepco), experienced a pipe failure at the Chalk Point Generating Station in southeastern Prince George's County, Maryland. (See figure 1 for a map showing the location of the Chalk Point Generating Station and the spill site.) The release was not discovered and addressed by the contract operating company, Support Terminal Services, Inc., (ST Services) until the late afternoon. Approximately 140,400 gallons[1] of fuel oil were released into the surrounding wetlands and Swanson Creek and, subsequently, the Patuxent River as a result of the accident. No injuries were caused by the accident, which cost approximately $71 million for environmental response and clean-up operations.

The Accident

At the time of the accident, Pepco was the owner of the Piney Point Oil Pipeline system. ST Services, a limited partnership of the Kaneb Pipe Line Company, operated the pipeline and performed certain maintenance functions according to the terms of its contract with Pepco.[2] The pipeline was used to deliver heated No. 6 fuel oil from Piney Point Terminal, in Maryland, through an intermediate station at Ryceville, Maryland, to Pepco's power generating stations at either Chalk Point or Morgantown, Maryland. (See figure 2.)

On April 7, 2000, a pigging operation was being conducted on the pipeline to prepare the Chalk Point Station to Ryceville Station segment of the pipeline for an in-line inspection. The pipeline from the Chalk Point Station to the Ryceville Station was started in the reverse direction of normal flow with flushing oil[3] in the system. (See figure 3 for a schematic of the pipeline.) Employees calculated the amount of oil in the Chalk Point flushing oil tank and the Ryceville receiving tank before the operation began. As the operation proceeded, they obtained tank level data that would typically be used to determine how much oil had been pumped from Chalk Point and how much had been received by Ryceville.

---

[1] Pipeline operators typically quantify their product using barrels rather than gallons. There are 42 gallons in a barrel.

[2] In December 2000, Pepco sold some of its facilities, including the Piney Point Oil Pipeline and the Chalk Point Generating Station, to Southern Energy, Inc., of Atlanta, Georgia. Southern Energy later became Mirant Mid-Atlantic of Atlanta, Georgia. Currently, Mirant Piney Point, LLP, (Mirant) is the pipeline owner and operator.

[3] *Flushing oil* is a mixture of No. 2 and No. 6 fuel oil. No. 6 fuel oil is a thick, black petroleum liquid that may become solid at cooler temperatures. No. 2 fuel oil is a light, refined petroleum product similar to diesel fuel.

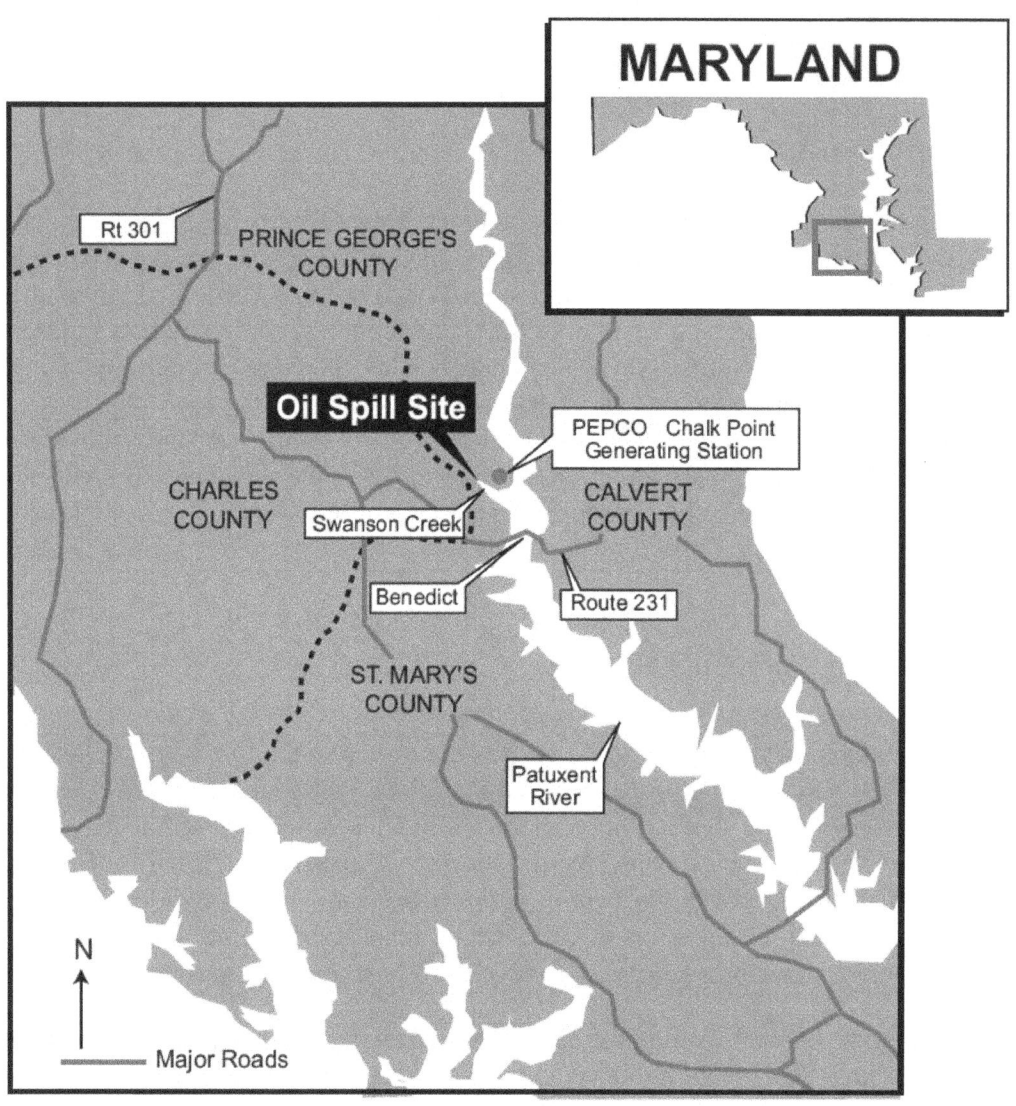

Figure 1. Map of accident site.

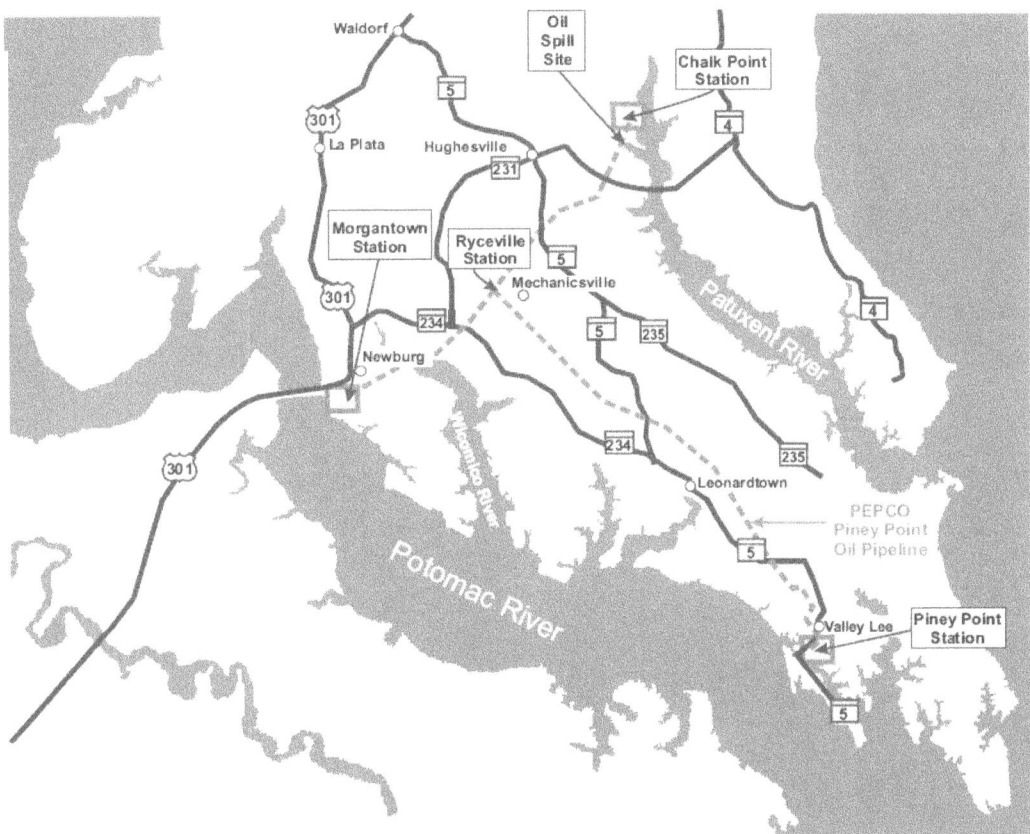

Figure 2. Locations of Piney Point Oil Pipeline Stations.

At 0715 eastern daylight time, ST Services employees (see figure 4) at the Chalk Point Station started pumping and launched a cleaning pig. Before this operation began, the estimated tank level that would indicate completion of the pigging process was calculated for Chalk Point. The first pig was initially estimated to arrive at the Ryceville Station 7 hours after it had been launched. Before launching the cleaning pig, the ST Services Chalk Point operator walked through the tank and pipe manifold area and measured the actual level[4] of the flushing oil tank. Within 15 to 25 minutes, a sizing pig[5] was launched to follow the cleaning pig.

The ST Services Chalk Point operator measured the first tank level at 0910. He passed this information on to the crew at Ryceville, who had the tank volume conversion tables that were used to determine the volume in the tank and calculate the oil flow rate. The first tank gauge was read at Ryceville shortly after the crew arrived, about 0837. The

---

[4] An operator obtains precise tank level measurements by climbing to the top of a tank carrying a weighted tape, which is used to determine the liquid level in the tank.

[5] The *sizing pig* was constructed to 90 percent of the pipeline's internal diameter to verify that the pipeline did not have any internal restrictions that could damage or restrict the passage of an ultrasonic inspection tool.

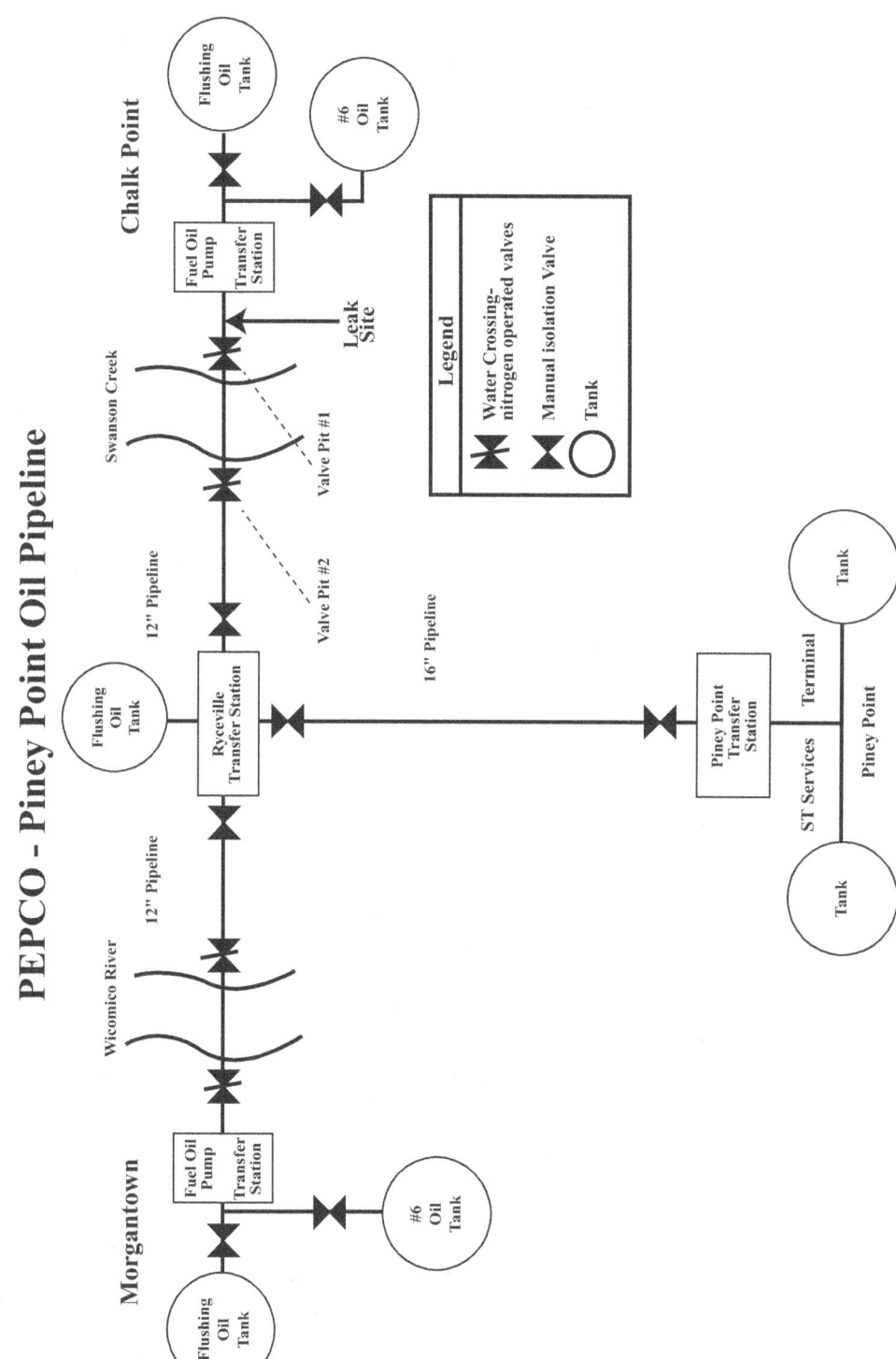

Figure 3. Piney Point Pipeline schematic.

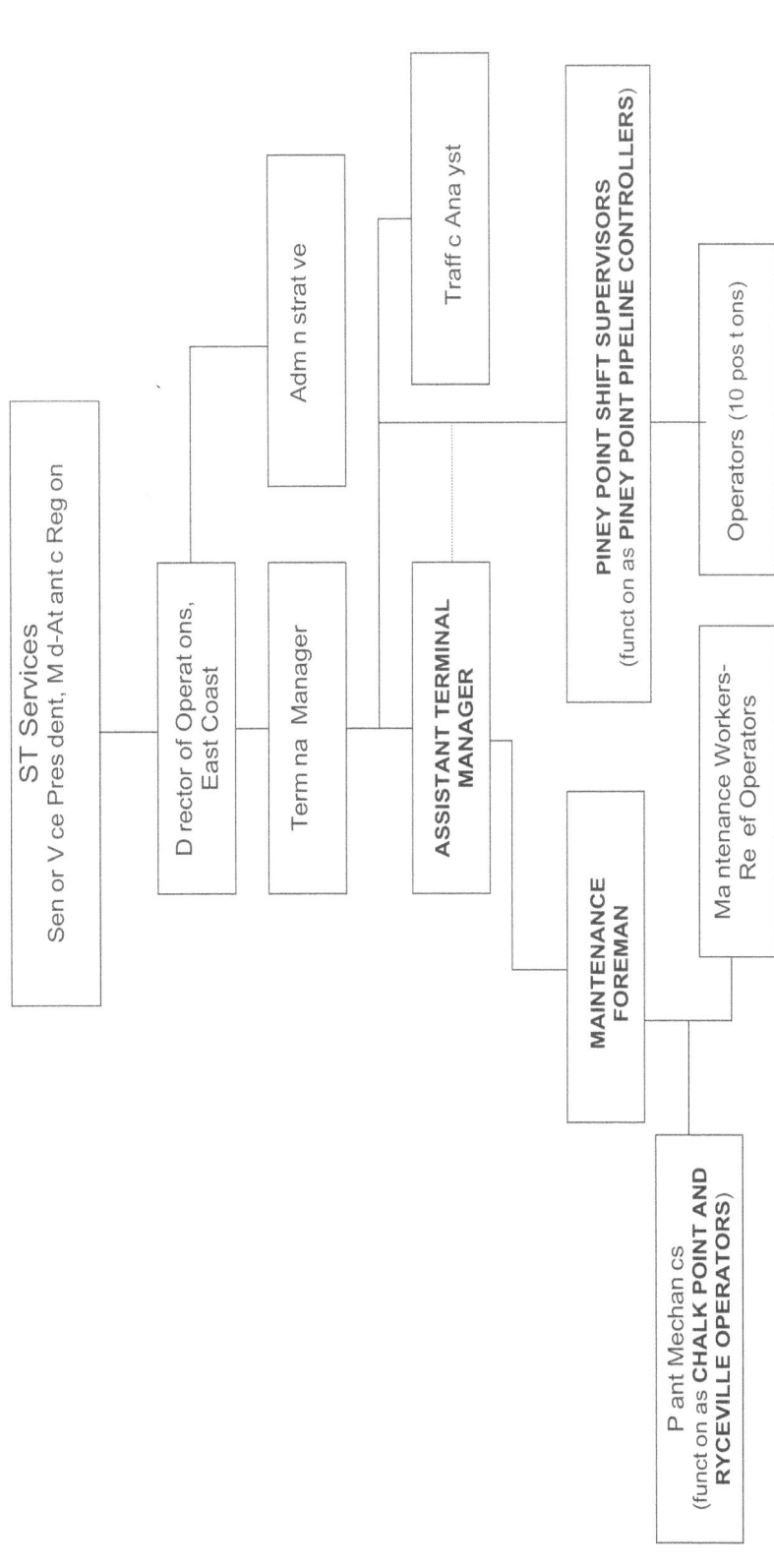

Figure 4. Selective organizational chart for ST Services. Positions cited in accident narrative are in boldface and all capitals. (Note: This chart was developed by the Safety Board for informational purposes. It is not intended to cover the full range of ST Services positions.)

ST Services Ryceville operator determined that about 1,500 barrels (63,000 gallons) had been transferred into the Ryceville tank since the pumping started. The ST Services Ryceville operator kept some notes during the pumping but did not record the time and tank level information in the station log.

Tank levels were taken at Chalk Point to be used to check the flow rate from the facility at about 2-hour intervals for most of the pumping operation. The ST Services Ryceville operator said he read the tank gauge at Ryceville, the receiving station, about every 1 1/2 hours to determine the volume of product in the Ryceville tank. The operating personnel did not provide tank volumes to the ST Services Chalk Point operator, and they did not calculate the line balance[6] periodically during the pigging operation. Further, they did not communicate the tank level information to the ST Services Piney Point pipeline controller[7] when it was obtained.

At 1119, another tank level measurement was made at Chalk Point, and the ST Services Chalk Point operator passed the information on to the ST Services Ryceville operator. A few minutes before 1200, the ST Services Chalk Point operator told Ryceville that the pumping was going well and that the cleaning pig would arrive early, between 1300 and 1330. At the same time, the ST Services Chalk Point operator asked Ryceville what it was getting for volume received, as he had not had any confirmation on the product pumped from his station to Ryceville. Ryceville told him the station was working on it. As a normal check-in, the ST Services Chalk Point operator also called the ST Services Piney Point pipeline controller to inform him that he was at the station and that things were going fine.

The next Chalk Point tank level measurement was taken at 1220 and reported to Ryceville and Piney Point. The ST Services Chalk Point operator stood by the Chalk Point pump starting about 1250 and was prepared to shut it down whenever he received a call from Ryceville stating that the cleaning pig had arrived. The tank gauge was checked at Ryceville about 1300, but no information on the volume received was calculated or reported to the ST Services Chalk Point operator or the ST Services Piney Point pipeline controller. The ST Services Ryceville operator went outside to the Ryceville pipe manifold about 1300 to await the cleaning pig's arrival. About 1412, the ST Services Chalk Point operator decided to double-check the Chalk Point tank level because the pig had not arrived at Ryceville.

About 1430, the Chalk Point pump started cavitating[8] due to a low-pressure condition at the pump inlet, because the level of product in the tank was not providing sufficient pressure for the pump to run properly. About the same time, the ST Services Ryceville operator noticed that Ryceville's meter noise suddenly stopped, indicating no

---

[6] *Line balance* is the difference between the volume of product pumped at the origin and the volume received at the destination. It is used for determining whether the pipeline operation is being conducted within certain limits in order to identify a possible leak.

[7] The ST Services Piney Point shift supervisors served as the pipeline controllers.

[8] *Cavitation* is an internal pump condition created by the sudden formation and collapse of bubbles in a liquid, which makes a characteristic sound.

product flow. The ST Services Chalk Point operator kept the pump operating by partially closing the pump outlet valve in an effort to avoid internal damage to the pump.

The ST Services Chalk Point operator talked to the ST Services maintenance foreman at Ryceville and was told that the meter noise had stopped and no pig had arrived. The ST Services Chalk Point operator was then directed to close the valve as much as possible to maintain product flow. The ST Services Chalk Point operator had not taken a recent tank level measurement but was now ordered by the ST Services maintenance foreman to determine the Chalk Point tank level. The ST Services Ryceville operator was also directed to measure the Ryceville tank level so that the volume pumped could be compared with the volume received. The ST Services assistant terminal manager was notified about the situation, and he confirmed the need for an immediate tank level measurement of the pumping and receiving tanks.

The ST Services Chalk Point operator and the ST Services assistant terminal manager had a phone conversation about 1440 and reviewed the situation. The ST Services assistant terminal manager instructed the ST Services Chalk Point operator to double-check which valves were closed to confirm that the No. 6 fuel system was isolated from the flushing oil system.

Tank levels were acquired for Chalk Point and Ryceville. The ST Services Ryceville operator, using the tank volume tables, calculated that enough oil had been pumped for the pigs to have reached the Ryceville Station. He said he thought that something was wrong because Ryceville did not receive all the oil pumped from Chalk Point.

The ST Services assistant terminal manager later said that at the time he believed that the tank volume discrepancy had been caused by a valve that was improperly aligned (open to another tank) or leaking (product leaking through a valve to another tank) and that flushing oil was being transferred to the No. 6 fuel oil tank. He then directed ST Services employees to make a number of checks to confirm that the correct valves were open, to obtain a reading of the No. 6 fuel oil meters at Chalk Point, and to measure the tanks at Piney Point. The ST Services assistant terminal manager had the ST Services Piney Point pipeline controller perform the line balance calculations, with the result that 3,088.7 barrels (129,725 gallons) could not be accounted for.

By 1534, after receiving the additional information he had requested, the ST Services assistant terminal manager stated that the discrepancies could not be explained by tank inventory data. He had ruled out the possibility of the missing oil being anywhere it should be. During a phone call, the ST Services Chalk Point operator told the ST Services assistant terminal manager that the requested check had confirmed the isolation of the flushing oil system from the No. 6 fuel oil. The ST Services assistant terminal manager told the ST Services Chalk Point operator to shut the Chalk Point pump down. At 1538, the ST Services Chalk Point operator shut down the pump. The ST Services assistant terminal manager stated that he paged his Pepco pipeline contact, the Pepco Chalk Point general supervisor for fuel and ash, three times using a "911 code" to indicate the urgent need for a response. (See figure 5 for an organizational chart of Pepco personnel involved in the accident.)

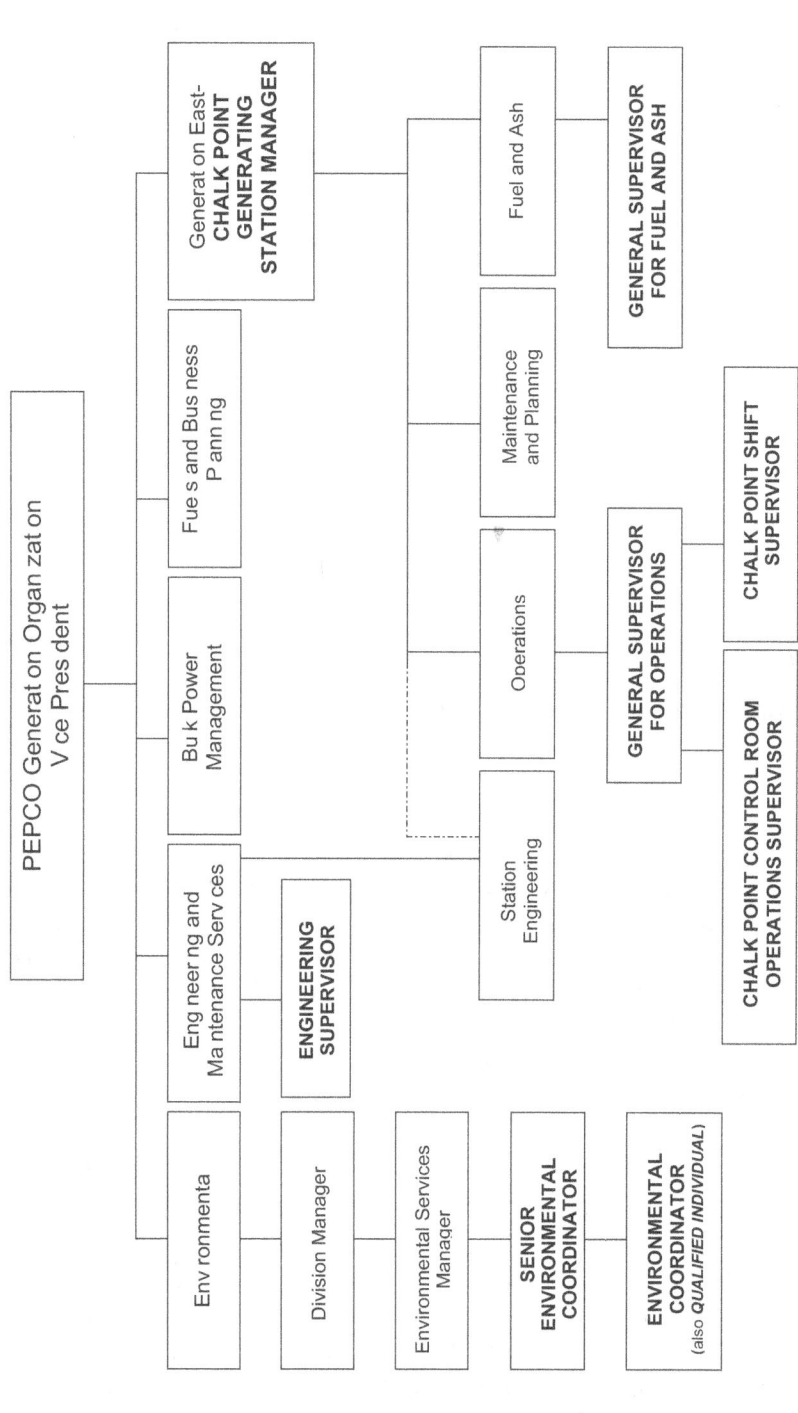

Figure 5. Selective and simplified organization chart for Pepco Generation Organization, intended only to show the basic organizational relationships between the major positions cited in the accident narrative. Positions cited in the narrative are in boldface and all capitals. (Note: This chart was developed by the Safety Board for informational purposes. It is not intended to cover the full range of Pepco Generation Organization positions.)

Actions Taken After Pipeline Shutdown

The ST Services assistant terminal manager told the ST Services Chalk Point operator that he had pumped about 8,900 barrels (373,800 gallons) and that Ryceville had received about 5,900 barrels (247,800 gallons). The ST Services assistant terminal manager then directed the ST Services Chalk Point operator to check the No. 1 valve pit area at Swanson Creek for a leak and to look across the creek at the No. 2 valve pit for signs of a leak. (Valve pit No. 1 is on the north side of Swanson Creek, between the creek and the Chalk Point Station.) The ST Services Chalk Point operator also obtained the closing tank level for the Chalk Point flushing oil tank.

The ST Services Chalk Point operator made the visual checks by 1545 and reported that he saw no sign of an oil leak at the creek. Next, the ST Services Chalk Point operator was directed to check all roads that the pipeline crossed back to Ryceville for an oil leak. He called the Chalk Point Operations Center and stated that he was finished pumping and that the pigs had not been received at Ryceville, indicating there was a problem with the pipeline. He said he told the Chalk Point Operations Center that he was checking road crossings and would contact the center if he noticed a leak or some other problem.

At 1550, the ST Services assistant terminal manager called a Pepco Washington, D.C., headquarters oil procurement employee who confirmed the pager number for the Pepco Chalk Point general supervisor for fuel and ash. The contact also provided the Pepco engineering supervisor's phone number, because the Pepco engineering supervisor might be able to locate other contacts needed by the ST Services assistant terminal manager.

The ST Services assistant terminal manager contacted the Pepco engineering supervisor, who advised him that the Pepco Chalk Point general supervisor for fuel and ash was on vacation. The ST Services assistant terminal manager told him the details of the 3,000-barrel line balance discrepancy and was advised to call the Pepco Chalk Point general supervisor for operations. The ST Services assistant terminal manager also stated that ST Services personnel were checking the levels of the flushing oil and No. 6 fuel oil tanks at Chalk Point, Morgantown, and Piney Point to determine the location of a 3,000-barrel line balance discrepancy. The ST Services assistant terminal manager indicated that similar discrepancies had occurred in the past due to valve misalignment or valves not being fully closed, which allowed oil to be inadvertently directed into one of the other oil storage tanks in the system.

The Pepco engineering supervisor said that about 1620, he called the Pepco Chalk Point general supervisor for operations and informed him of a 2,000- to 3,000-barrel line balance discrepancy, which the Pepco Chalk Point general supervisor for operations noted in his log as a discrepancy of 2,000 barrels. The Pepco Chalk Point general supervisor for operations also noted in his log that ST Services personnel had initiated a ground inspection and were checking the pipeline at road crossings. At 1643, the Pepco Chalk Point general supervisor for operations ordered a patrol flight of the pipeline right-of-way.

Response to Accident

Notifying Authorities and Containing Spill

April 7. About 1800 or shortly thereafter, the Pepco Chalk Point general supervisor for operations called the on-duty Pepco environmental coordinator, who was the designated Pepco qualified individual,[9] at home to discuss the pipeline line balance shortage. He told the Pepco qualified individual what was being done at the pipeline, including the tank level measurement discrepancy found when oil had been pumped back to Ryceville. The Pepco Chalk Point general supervisor for operations also said that he had ordered a pipeline patrol flight.

At 1802, the ST Services assistant terminal manager learned that during the pipeline patrol plane flight, an oil release from the Piney Point Oil Pipeline had been spotted in the Swanson Creek wetlands area. By 1807, the ST Services assistant terminal manager had put the Chalk Point pipeline emergency response plan into effect by contacting the Pepco qualified individual and an oil spill clean-up contractor. This plan listed the criteria for notification of local response agencies as "fire, explosion, personal injury or release or significant threat of release off-site." Local response agencies were not notified. The ST Services assistant terminal manager called Piney Point to summon ST Services employees to assist at Chalk Point. (See appendix B for a timeline indicating significant developments as the leak occurred and was identified.)

The Pepco qualified individual called the Pepco Chalk Point general supervisor for operations back and reported that the pipeline patrol flight had found an oil spill. The Pepco Chalk Point general supervisor for operations then notified the Chalk Point control room of the pipeline release.

The Pepco Chalk Point general supervisor for operations sent the Pepco Chalk Point shift supervisor to the pipeline crossing at Swanson Creek to assess the situation. During this period, the Pepco Chalk Point general supervisor for operations reviewed the three Pepco spill response plans for the area to ensure that all emergency response requirements were being met.[10] Because each plan had a somewhat different purpose and focus and the general supervisor for operations did not know the exact location of the (underground) spill, he did not know which plan applied to this accident. Consequently, he attempted to notify all response personnel identified in all three plans.

---

[9] As indicated under 49 *Code of Federal Regulations* (CFR) Part 194, the *qualified individual* is a company representative available on a 24-hour basis with full authority to: activate personnel and contract with required oil spill removal organization(s); activate personnel and equipment maintained by the operator; act as liaison with the on-scene coordinator; and obligate funds needed to carry out all required or directed oil response activities.

[10] The three plans were 1) the *Pepco Oil Spill Emergency Response Plan for the Ryceville Pumping Station and Pipeline*, 2) the *Pepco Oil Spill Emergency Response Plan for the Chalk Point Generating Station*, and 3) the *Pepco Spill Prevention, Control, and Emergency Response Plan for the Chalk Point Generating Station*.

About 1817, the Pepco Chalk Point shift supervisor called the Pepco Chalk Point general supervisor for operations and reported that he would deploy an oil spill boom to contain the oil in Swanson Creek.

At 1822, the ST Services assistant terminal manager asked the Pepco Chalk Point control room operations supervisor to notify Federal and State agencies about the release, as required by the oil spill response plan for the Chalk Point Generating Station. About 1827, the Pepco Chalk Point general supervisor for operations called the headquarters Pepco senior environmental coordinator at home and discussed the oil spill, so that the Pepco senior environmental coordinator could notify the National Response Center.[11]

Between 1830 and 1835, the Pepco qualified individual met the Pepco Chalk Point shift supervisor (who had been to the leak site) at the Chalk Point plant building and asked the shift supervisor how much oil had spilled. When the Pepco Chalk Point shift supervisor responded that he was not sure, the Pepco qualified individual pressed him for some number because, he said, he believed that he would have to report a spill quantity when he called the responsible authorities. The Pepco qualified individual stated that, when pressed, the Pepco Chalk Point shift supervisor said, "1,000 gallons, 2,000 gallons, [expletive] mess; tell them what you want."

They reported together to the office of the Pepco Chalk Point general supervisor for operations about 1835, during his continuing telephone conversation with the Pepco senior environmental coordinator. The Pepco qualified individual told the Pepco Chalk Point general supervisor for operations that the estimated size of the spill was 1,000 to 2,000 gallons. The Pepco senior environmental coordinator later told investigators that during their phone conversation, he and the Pepco Chalk Point general supervisor for operations discussed that the "best guess" estimate of the release was 1,000 to 2,000 gallons. He stated that he and the Pepco Chalk Point general supervisor for operations agreed to report a release of 2,000 gallons to the National Response Center. The Pepco senior environmental coordinator stated that the Pepco Chalk Point general supervisor for operations did not discuss the ST Services tank level readings with him.

Shortly thereafter, the Pepco senior environmental coordinator called the Pepco qualified individual for more information about the release. The Pepco qualified individual confirmed the oil spill location and stated that booms were being placed in the wetlands. Based on the information they had, the Pepco senior environmental coordinator and the Pepco qualified individual decided to report the estimated spill volume as 2,000 gallons. They agreed to split the reporting task, with the Pepco senior environmental coordinator reporting to the National Response Center and the Pepco qualified individual reporting to the Maryland Department of the Environment.

---

[11] The *National Response Center* serves as the communications hub of the *National Response System*, which is the Federal Government's mechanism for providing emergency responses to discharges of oil and releases of chemicals. The National Response Center receives reports of all reportable oil and hazardous substance releases anywhere in the United States and its territories. The National Response Center then distributes incident reports to predetermined Government agencies based on National Response Center incident classification guidelines.

Around 1840, the Pepco Chalk Point general supervisor for operations received a call from the ST Services assistant terminal manager, who advised him that the ST Services tank level readings were 3,000 barrels (126,000 gallons) short, that the spill covered 3 to 4 acres in the wetlands at Swanson Creek, and that he had activated an oil spill contractor. He also said that ST Services personnel would be arriving in about 15 minutes to close the pipeline valve between Swanson Creek and the Ryceville Station. The notes made by the Pepco Chalk Point general supervisor for operations at this time recorded the figure of "3,000 barrels" and that a 3- to 4-acre area was affected by the release.

At 1845, the Pepco qualified individual called the Maryland Department of the Environment to report the release. At 1850, the Pepco qualified individual called the Pepco Chalk Point general supervisor for operations and told him that he had reported a 2,000-gallon release to the Maryland Department of the Environment.

About 1850, the Pepco senior environmental coordinator called the National Response Center and reported a 2,000-gallon No. 2 fuel oil release from a pipeline at the Pepco Chalk Point Generating Station, on the border of the facility property where the pipeline crosses Swanson Creek. The Pepco senior environmental coordinator stated that he understood from people at the plant that most or all of the release was in the creek. The Pepco senior environmental coordinator also reported that the incident was discovered at 1817 on Friday, April 7, and that a clean up and an investigation into the cause of the accident were underway. The Pepco senior environmental coordinator indicated that Pepco had booms in the creek, that materials to absorb oil were being used, and that clean-up contractors had been activated. He reported that he was not aware of any injuries or evacuations. The National Response Center watch officer designated the release notification as Incident Report No. 525411 and, lacking information on the exact source of the leak, inaccurately classified it as a fixed (power plant) facility incident rather than a pipeline-type incident. The National Response Center officer sent notifications to the agencies on the fixed facility distribution list.[12] Following the Pepco senior environmental coordinator's notification of the National Response Center, the Pepco qualified individual notified the U.S. Coast Guard Marine Safety Office in Baltimore, Maryland.

By 1850, the Pepco spill response teams had completed the initial deployment of more than 1 mile of floating boom in the wetland area on the north side of Swanson Creek and at the mouth of Swanson Creek on the Patuxent River.

About 1911, the National Response Center notified Environmental Protection Agency (EPA) Region III (Philadelphia) of the accident by fax.[13] About 1930, the on-call EPA Federal On-Scene Coordinator for Region III contacted the Prince George's County Fire Department requesting directions to the site and was advised that Prince George's County had not been notified of the spill.

---

[12] The National Response Center maintains a number of distribution lists. The Office of Pipeline Safety was on the pipeline accident distribution list but not the fixed facility accident distribution list.

[13] The EPA responds to spills in the inland areas of the United States, and the Coast Guard responds to spills in U.S. coastal and inland waterways.

The EPA Federal On-Scene Coordinator contacted the Pepco senior environmental coordinator and advised him to call the Prince George's County Communication Center and provide the spill information. The Pepco senior environmental coordinator contacted the Prince George's County Communications Center and advised the center that "2,000 gallons of No. 2 fuel oil was released and county fire response was not necessary." The communications center informed the county's hazardous materials coordinator about the spill, and the hazardous materials coordinator arrived at the accident site within 15 minutes to assess the situation.

About 2015, the Pepco qualified individual stated that when he returned to the Chalk Point command center, he learned from the information blackboard that the estimated spill volume was 3,000 barrels (126,000 gallons), rather than 2,000 gallons. The Pepco qualified individual stated that he advised Maryland Department of the Environment and Coast Guard representatives, following their arrival on the scene about 2030, that the spill was "closer to 3,000 barrels in quantity." Shortly afterwards, this information was relayed to the Coast Guard Baltimore office and the State emergency response duty officer. At 2035, the responders from the Maryland Department of the Environment called their emergency response duty officer and advised him that the updated release amount was 3,000 barrels.

Between 2030 and 2100, outside response personnel (including spill response contractors, key Pepco responders, and State and Federal personnel) began arriving with additional boom and boom deployment boats to augment those that Pepco already had at the site. Around 2050, ST Services and other contractors working under Pepco's direction began evacuating oil from the pipeline between the closed No. 1 river pit valve and the Chalk Point Pump Station.

Shortly after 2100, members of Pepco's engineering and maintenance services group confirmed a 3,000-barrel release, based on calculations using the tank level readings that ST Services used. The Pepco senior environmental coordinator stated that, when he arrived at the Chalk Point command center about 2130, he learned from the information blackboard that the release volume was estimated to be 3,000 barrels (126,000 gallons). The Pepco senior environmental coordinator stated that even though he had notified several agencies earlier of the 2,000-gallon amount, he did not revise the 2,000-gallon notification because he believed representatives of all the agencies he had notified were on-scene or in contact with each other.

Around 2300, Pepco conducted a command post briefing, during which participants reviewed the boom placement and the need to augment the boom Pepco had already deployed to contain the oil. They agreed for the night to place booms to direct the oil to a point accessible to a vacuum truck. The command post briefing also covered plans for deploying additional boom at 0600 on April 8, before the anticipated tide change. During the remainder of the night, Coast Guard Baltimore office representatives and the Maryland Department of the Environment on-scene coordinator worked with Pepco and its spill response contractors to contain the spill and prepare collection efforts.

April 8. Shortly after 0115, a member of the Prince George's County Hazardous Materials Team contacted the National Response Center watch officer and advised the watch officer to update the Coast Guard Baltimore office about the accident status. He also asked the watch officer whether the Chalk Point event constituted a transportation-related incident requiring notification of the U.S. Department of Transportation's Office of Pipeline Safety. Subsequently, the National Response Center determined that the accident was a pipeline incident rather than a fixed facility incident and distributed the original incident report, containing the 2,000-gallon spill estimate, to its pipeline notification list, including the Office of Pipeline Safety and the Safety Board.

Around 0250, the Coast Guard Federal on-scene representative arrived at the accident site to coordinate Federal, State, and local efforts. The Coast Guard representative provided Pepco with a copy of the Baltimore Area Contingency Plan and discussed with Pepco representatives the possibility of pre-staging booms at environmentally sensitive creeks identified under the area contingency plan. After assessing the spill location, the Coast Guard representative notified the Coast Guard Baltimore office that the spill was located above the Benedict Bridge on Highway 231. According to the Baltimore Area Contingency Plan, Benedict Bridge marks the jurisdictional dividing line between the Coast Guard Baltimore office and the EPA's Region III. Had the spill passed under Benedict Bridge, it would have been considered within the Coast Guard's geographic jurisdiction.

Around 0330, the Coast Guard Baltimore office notified EPA Region III that the spill was in the EPA's geographic jurisdiction and that Coast Guard personnel were responding. Several hours later, when the Coast Guard representative on-scene was able to view the wetlands area in daylight, he updated the Coast Guard Baltimore office. Shortly after 0530, the Coast Guard Baltimore office advised the EPA Federal On-Scene Coordinator that although the Coast Guard had personnel on the scene, the EPA should take the lead for the spill, because the spill was contained in the wetlands and it had significantly contaminated the wetlands area, including the local wildlife, with oil.

Shortly after 0600, the EPA Federal On-Scene Coordinator deployed from Philadelphia with an EPA technical support contractor. Around 1015, the EPA Federal On-Scene Coordinator arrived at the site and assumed responsibility from the Coast Guard for directing the clean-up activity. Soon afterwards, the EPA Federal On-Scene Coordinator learned for the first time that the quantity of oil released was actually 3,000 barrels, rather than 2,000 gallons, of a mixture of No. 2 and No. 6 fuel oil. About 1100, the EPA Federal On-Scene Coordinator held an organizational meeting with representatives of all the parties, including Pepco, Pepco's three spill response contractors,[14] the Maryland Department of the Environment, the Coast Guard, and the U.S. Fish and Wildlife Service. At the meeting, those attending agreed that:

---

[14] The contractors were A&A Environmental Services, Wood Chuck Enterprise, and Clean Harbors (standby contactor).

- The Unified Command (the EPA, the Maryland Department of the Environment, and Pepco) would direct the management of the response effort.[15]

- The responders would continue with the existing boom placement. The containment and clean-up efforts appeared to be effective, and there was no apparent threat to public health.

- Because of the large amount of free product in the wetlands, the primary emphasis should be on collection of oil in advance of a storm expected by early evening.

- With the spill contained in the wetlands, the Unified Command would release the standby contractor, Clean Harbors.

The weather forecasts changed throughout the afternoon. Earlier forecasts tended to indicate the approach of a relatively weak storm, but the weather reports became more threatening as the day progressed. Around 1600, and with the expected approach of severe winds and heavy rains, the EPA and the Maryland Department of the Environment surveyed Pepco's site response activities and revised the storm plan so that additional collection resources were placed at the secondary containment points and outer booms.

During the early stages of the response, Pepco deployed about 300 of its own employees and spill response contractors to assist with the oil recovery efforts. (See figure 6.) Pepco response personnel were on rotating 8-hour shifts. The EPA Federal On-Scene Coordinator noted that those coming on shift typically were not briefed before or after arriving at the scene. Little information was shared between shifts of employees. Pepco response officials stated that they often were not included in the meetings conducted by the EPA Federal On-Scene Coordinator. In some cases, they could not attend such meetings because it was physically impossible; the space provided for the meetings was inadequate to accommodate all those wishing to attend. Pepco indicated that because of these problems with the meetings, some of the orders of the Unified Command were not clearly communicated to its personnel.[16] At the same time, some meeting attendees were not essential to the response effort.

---

[15] A *Unified Command* is an element within the Incident Command System that represents the key organizations responding to the incident. Under the National Contingency Plan, the Unified Command typically consists of the Federal On-Scene Coordinator, the State on-scene coordinator, and the incident commander of the responsible party.

[16] From a letter, dated August 3, 2000, from Pepco's incident commander for the Chalk Point response to the EPA Federal On-Scene Coordinator for the response concerning lessons learned from the emergency response to the Chalk Point oil spill.

Because Pepco's qualified individual changed with every 8-hour shift, the Pepco qualified individual did not provide continuity of response and often had to check with other Pepco officials before providing assistance requested by the EPA Federal On-Scene Coordinator. In her postaccident description of events, the EPA Federal On-Scene Coordinator cited the frequent changing of Pepco's qualified individual and stated that it led to "episodes of miscommunication and unclear lines of authority during the initial key dates of the response."[17]

Figure 6. Response personnel working on wooden mats in the marsh.

During the first 24 hours of the spill response, three sets of booms had been deployed, and the oil spill was contained in about 5 acres of wetlands. However, during the evening of April 8, the weather deteriorated, and conditions included winds in excess of 50 mph and strong rain showers. Because of the heavy rains and high wind gusts, the outer booms were breached about 2030, releasing a significant amount of oil into the Patuxent River. (See figure 7 for an aerial photo of two plumes of oil in Swanson Creek, moving toward the Patuxent River.) During the night, Pepco's spill response contractors attempted to deploy additional personnel and equipment, but the weather made it unsafe for workers to be in the wetlands area or on the river, so they could not be deployed. (See appendix C for a listing of the significant events between the recognition of the leak and the loss of oil containment.)

---

[17] Environmental Protection Agency, *After-Action Report for Emergency Response at the Swanson Creek Oil Spill Site, Aquasco, Maryland, Prince George's, Charles, Calvert, and St. Mary's Counties 7 April 2000 to 16 May 2000*, p. 30.

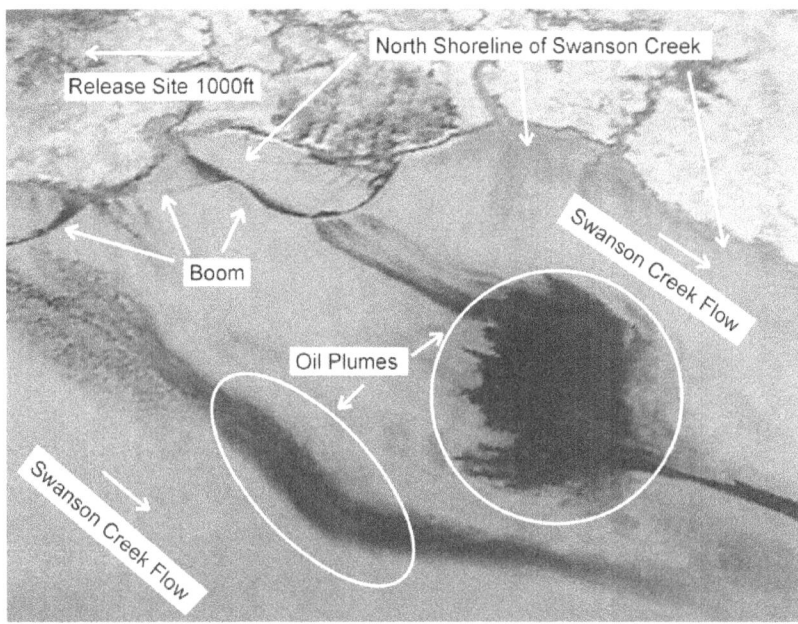

Figure 7. Aerial photo of Swanson Creek area taken on April 10, 2000 showing two plumes of oil moving with the creek flow towards the Patuxent River after containment was lost.

Response to Escape From Containment

After the storm caused the oil to escape containment on the evening of April 8, the Unified Command attempted, primarily using Pepco contractor resources, to reestablish control over the spill. The efforts were unsuccessful until the Unified Command 1) obtained additional personnel to implement an Incident Command System structure on April 11, and 2) obtained additional marine response equipment for oil recovery. Between April 8 and 12, the oil plume spread approximately 17 miles (linear) downstream, affecting approximately 40 miles of shoreline, including several environmentally sensitive and populated creeks in Calvert and St. Mary's Counties. (See figure 8 for creek boom locations and spread of spill.) The major events that took place during the response to the oil's escape from containment are provided below.

April 9. In the early daylight hours of April 9, an oil plume was observed traveling in a straight line from the mouth of Swanson Creek across the Patuxent River towards Calvert County. At 0745, the EPA Federal On-Scene Coordinator contacted the Baltimore office of the Coast Guard to state that the containment had failed and to ask the Coast Guard to identify potential Federal resources with marine capabilities. The Coast Guard directed the EPA Federal On-Scene Coordinator to several possible sources of assistance (Patuxent Naval Air Base, etc.) in the vicinity. Shortly thereafter, Pepco informed the EPA Federal On-Scene Coordinator that it was having difficulty obtaining the necessary contractor resources with marine capabilities, particularly the waterborne skimmers and skimming vessels needed to respond effectively.

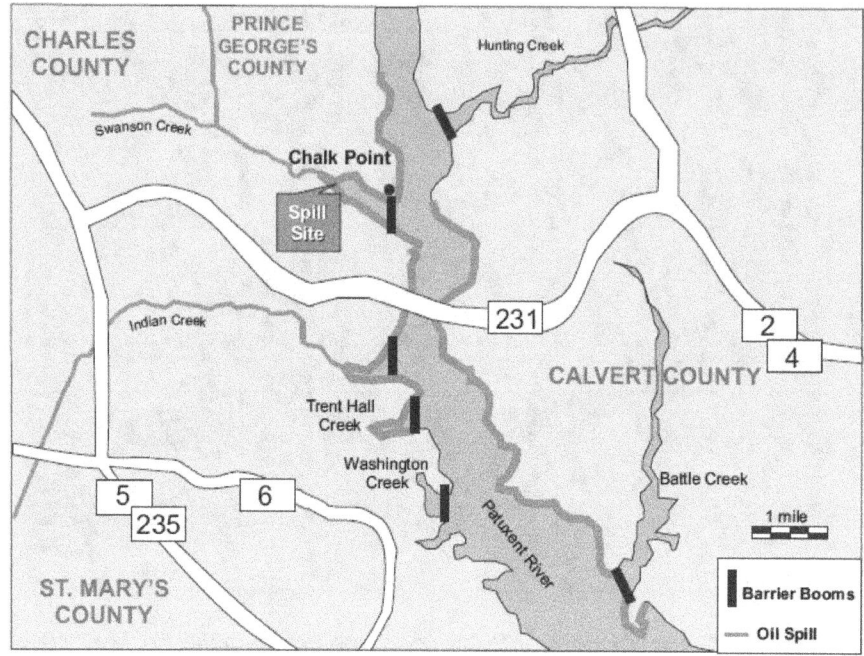

Figure 8. Spill site map showing creek boom placements and range of oil spill.

As the morning progressed, Pepco's contractors were deployed in an effort to corral the moving oil plume on the river with booms before it could affect the Calvert County shoreline. The effort was unsuccessful.

By mid-afternoon, the EPA Federal On-Scene Coordinator, other EPA officials on the scene, the Maryland Department of the Environment on-scene coordinator, and a U.S. Department of the Interior representative had met and agreed that the spill represented a substantial threat to public health and the environment. As a result, the EPA contracted with the Marine Spill Response Corporation, an environmental spill response contractor, to provide on-water response services and personnel.[18]

At 2100, another meeting was held, during which the protective booming of the environmentally sensitive Hunting, Indian, and Trent Hall Creeks, all of which fed into the Patuxent River, was given a high priority. As a result, it was decided to continue contractor response efforts through the night.

April 10. Around 1200, the EPA Federal On-Scene Coordinator and the Maryland Department of the Environment on-scene coordinator toured the accident site with the

---

[18] The Marine Spill Response Corporation is a not-for-profit organization that is funded by member companies. It allows only the Federal Government or member companies to hire it to respond to spills involving releases greater than 1,200 barrels. Pepco was not a member company.

Pepco qualified individual and expressed concern that 1) Pepco's spill response contractors had not completed booming the threatened creeks according to plans, 2) the contractors were making ineffective use of the available response resources, and 3) the reports being provided to the Unified Command by Pepco about the progress of the response effort were inaccurate. In recognition of the problems, at 1430, the EPA Federal On-Scene Coordinator asked Coast Guard on-site personnel to develop an Incident Command System structure for the response, under her direction. About the same time, the EPA Federal On-Scene Coordinator strongly advised Pepco that it had to greatly increase its logistical support for and control over the response contractors and that a spill management contractor was needed.

At the 2100 staff meeting, the EPA Federal On-Scene Coordinator stressed the need to deploy protective boom around the creeks. She directed Pepco to immediately deploy protective booms at Hunting, Indian, and Trent Hall Creeks. At 2200, the EPA Federal On-Scene Coordinator requested that the Coast Guard provide 25 employees by 0600 on April 11 to staff the Incident Command System structure that was being developed.

April 11. By 0300, the booming of the creeks had not been completed. The EPA Federal On-Scene Coordinator again directed Pepco to protectively boom the creeks. At 0715, an overflight of the affected area showed that no boom had been installed to protect the creeks and that Trent Hall and Indian Creeks both showed evidence of significant oil contamination.

At the 0900 meeting, Pepco indicated that it was attempting to bring additional contractor resources to the scene. The EPA Federal On-Scene Coordinator, in recognition of the "continued failure of the Pepco contractors to carry out direction from the Unified Command,"[19] began preparing to have additional Federal environmental responders participate in the Incident Command System structure.

The Coast Guard Captain of the Port of Baltimore arrived on the scene about 1100, with additional personnel to staff the Incident Command System structure that had been developed since the previous day. Organizational functions were split into four sections—operations, planning, logistics, and finance—and Unified Command officials managed each section. All field operations were carried out under the direction of the operations section. The newly arriving Coast Guard personnel were designated to monitor the field operations being conducted by Pepco's contractors to ensure that work was completed in a timely and efficient fashion.

The EPA Federal On-Scene Coordinator again asked Pepco to hire a spill management team to manage its contractors and the spill response. Pepco subsequently stated that a firm had been contracted to provide logistic management support and keep track of the contractor and equipment resources at the site.

---

[19] Environmental Protection Agency, *After-Action Report for Emergency Response at the Swanson Creek Oil Spill Site, Aquasco, Maryland, Prince George's, Charles, Calvert, and St. Mary's Counties, 7 April 2000 to 16 May 2000.* Appendix A, Incident Chronology, p. A-9.

During the remainder of the day, protective booming was provided for Hunting Creek, and protective boom was pre-staged for deployment on April 12 for four more creeks.

April 12 and Afterwards. Once the Incident Command System structure was implemented, recovery operations were conducted and monitored around the clock with day and night crews. Protective booms were provided for threatened creeks on April 12 and 13. Eventually, more than 1,000 contract workers were hired to assist with the clean-up operations.

Restrictions on boating were imposed, and the Maryland Department of the Environment issued a precautionary advisory on the harvest and consumption of fish and crabs from the contaminated areas on the Patuxent River. A rehabilitation center for wildlife was established for oiled animals.

By April 13, Marine Spill Response Corporation skimmers had completed the collection of free oil in the main body of the Patuxent River. Free oil continued to be collected through April 16 in several affected creeks in St. Mary's County. During the last few days of April 2000, the Unified Command developed a long-term site remediation plan addressing oil removal from the wetlands, soil treatment, site decontamination, and demobilization. On May 16, 2000, the Unified Command declared the emergency response phase over. (See appendix D for a timeline of the significant developments in the environmental response effort.)

Damage

Total environmental clean-up costs were approximately $71 million.

On April 24, 2000, the Maryland Department of the Environment lifted the advisories it had issued earlier against the harvest and consumption of products from the Patuxent River. Based on laboratory analyses of crab, fish, and shellfish samples, the Maryland Department of the Environment determined that eating these river products would not pose a significant potential for adverse human health effects. In addition, the Maryland Department of the Environment stated that it had determined that no permanent damage had been done to fishing resources as a result of the spill.

Personnel Information

The ST Services Chalk Point operator on the day of the accident was a plant mechanic with over 7 years' experience on the Piney Point Oil Pipeline. His duties included repairing pumps, valves, and construction equipment and being an equipment and pipeline operator when required. He reported to the ST Services maintenance foreman.

The ST Services Ryceville operator on the day of the accident was a plant mechanic with 7 years' experience on the Piney Point Oil Pipeline. His duties included repairing pumps, valves, and construction equipment and being an equipment and pipeline operator when required. He reported to the ST Services maintenance foreman.

The ST Services maintenance foreman had over 3 years' experience on the Piney Point Oil Pipeline. His duties included supervising five employees in terminal and pipeline operations and maintenance. He reported to the ST Services assistant terminal manager.

The ST Services assistant terminal manager started working at the Piney Point Terminal in 1973 in various positions, which included carrying out pipeline operations and maintenance responsibilities for the previous terminal owner. He had approximately 5 years' experience with ST Services as an assistant terminal manager with responsibilities for the Piney Point Terminal and the Piney Point Oil Pipeline. He reported to the Piney Point Terminal manager.

Postaccident Examination

The April 7, 2000, pipeline rupture occurred at the Chalk Point Generating Station in southeastern Prince George's County. At this location, the pipeline was on Pepco property and passed through wetlands adjacent to Swanson Creek, a tributary to the Patuxent River. The release point was 127 feet north of valve pit No. 1 on Pepco property.

The pipe at the failure area was 12 3/4-inch-diameter, 0.203-inch wall thickness, American Petroleum Institute (API) 5L grade X42 electric resistance weld steel pipe, installed with 1-inch polyurethane thermal insulation and a 170-mill polyethylene jacket exterior coating. The pipe was insulated and coated before the field bend at this location was made during the pipeline's installation.

The pipeline was buried about 3 1/2 feet deep at the rupture location. The rupture area was excavated a few days after the failure. When the pipeline was exposed, the profile of a buckle could be seen through the pipe coating. (See figure 9.) When the pipe coating was removed, a crack in the circumferential direction was visible.

In a postaccident communication from Pepco to Safety Board staff, Pepco stated it had reviewed the recorded pressure information, the size of the pipeline crack, and the pipeline operating conditions at the time of the accident and determined that, to release the estimated 129,000 gallons of product spilled, the pipe failure had to have occurred at least 5 hours before the Chalk Point pump began cavitating at 1430 on April 7, 2000. A subsequent communication from Mirant (current operator of the pipeline)[20] to Safety Board staff noted that the failure had probably occurred during the startup of the Chalk

---

[20] Pepco sold the Piney Point Oil Pipeline and the Chalk Point Generating Station in December 2000. Mirant subsequently became the pipeline owner and operator.

Point pump, about 0715, when pipeline pressure was at its highest. Mirant also indicated that the final estimated release quantity was about 3,343 barrels (140,400 gallons).

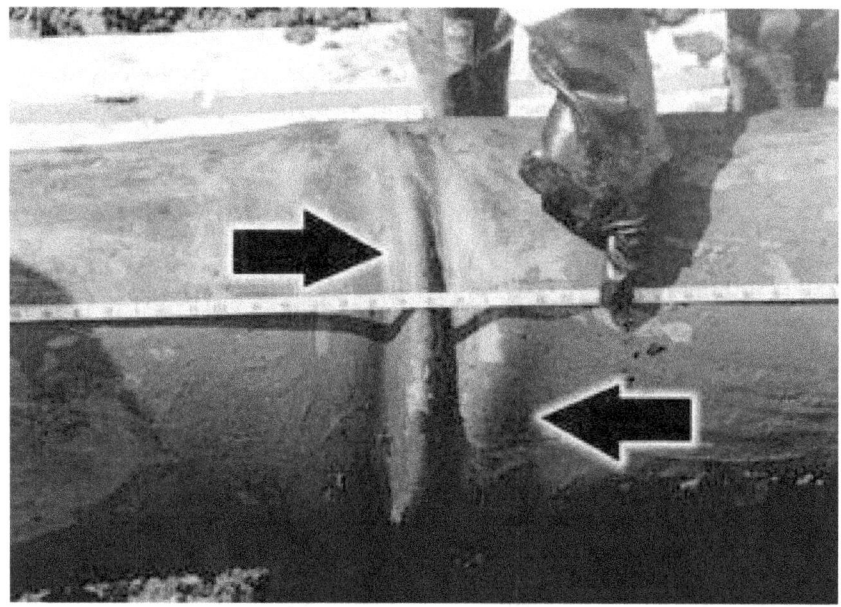

Figure 9. Indication of the buckle (Arrows show buckle location).

Tests and Research

A 53-inch-long section of pipeline taken from the scene was examined at the Safety Board laboratory. The pipe was bent and contained an outward-protruding buckle on the inside radius of the bend. The angle of the bend in which the buckle was formed was determined to be in the 5- to 6-degree range. The buckle extended around 270 degrees of the pipe circumference, from approximately the 10 o'clock to the 7 o'clock position. (See figure 10.) The pipe was deformed into a slightly elliptical shape. The buckle area contained an open crack at the crown of the buckle, which extended from approximately the 2 o'clock to the 4 o'clock position. The maximum height of the buckle was approximately 1 inch at the 3 o'clock position on the inside of the bend. The crack was 6 1/2-inches long by 3/8-inch wide at its widest portion. (See figure 11.) No external corrosion was noted on the pipe section when it was examined under a microscope.

The interior surface of the pipe in the area of the buckle peak contained a number of shallow secondary cracks. All the cracks were circumferentially oriented, confined to the permanently deformed area of the pipe (approximately 1/4 inch from the buckle apex), had blunt tips, and were filled with corrosion products. Some of these cracks exhibited slight branching. The appearance of these cracks was typical of corrosion fatigue cracking in low carbon steels, resulting from exposure to high stress amplitudes.

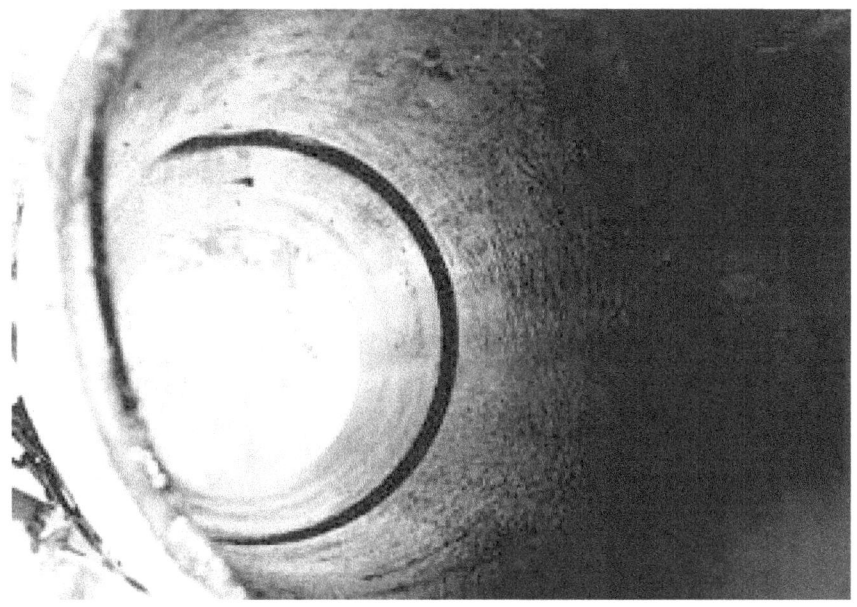

Figure 10. Inside view of the buckle in the removed section of pipe.

Figure 11. 6 1/2-inch-long, 3/8-inch-wide crack,
with coating system shown at the left edge of photo.

A scanning electron microscope examination revealed five well-defined fracture zones. Figure 12 illustrates the fracture surface profile of the failure. Bracket "a" starts at the interior surface of the pipe, showing a fracture from corrosion fatigue. Brackets "b," "c," and "d" show the crack propagation planes changing from 45 degrees from the surface of the pipe to roughly perpendicular, showing both tensile overstress and fatigue propagation, and contain no evidence of corrosion. Bracket "e" shows the crack propagation changing to a 45-degree shear plane. The final separation zone adjacent to the exterior surface of the pipe reveals dimpled features typical of ductile overstress fractures.

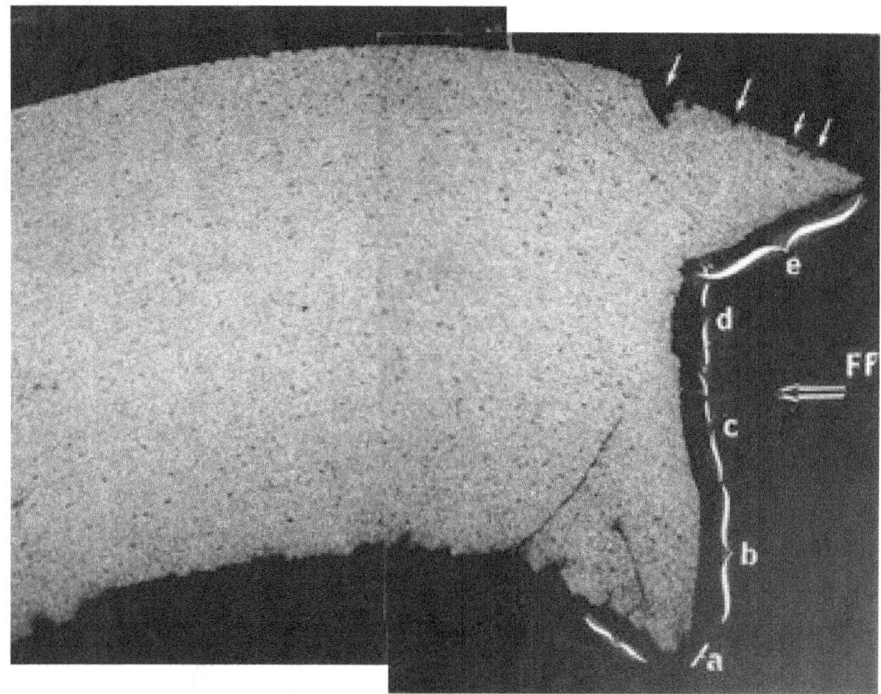

Figure 12. Fracture surface profile of failure.

Piney Point Oil Pipeline

Pipeline Information

The Piney Point Oil Pipeline was constructed for the Steuart Petroleum Company in 1971 and 1972 and put in service in 1973. Pepco purchased the pipeline in 1976. In 1995, ST Services purchased the Piney Point Terminal facility from Steuart Petroleum, and ST Services operated the pipeline for Pepco with former Steuart Petroleum personnel.

Fuel oil was delivered to the Piney Point Terminal by marine vessels and then transported from the terminal by the Piney Point Oil Pipeline. The 51.5-mile-long pipeline system was composed of 12-inch and 16-inch-diameter pipeline segments that were used to transport heated fuel oil from the Piney Point Terminal, via the intermediate Ryceville Station, to generating stations at Chalk Point and Morgantown. The pipeline segment from Ryceville to Chalk Point was approximately 11 miles long. The oil was heated to make it flow more easily, and the system operated up to approximately 160° F.

1995 In-line Inspection. The Ryceville to Chalk Point segment of the Piney Point Oil Pipeline was internally inspected in November 1995 with a geometry tool and an in-line magnetic flux leakage tool. After receiving the inspection reports in January 1996, Pepco exposed the pipeline and examined corrosion anomalies at 29 locations in spring 1996. The data from the magnetic flux inspection did not correlate well with field measurements for either wall loss data or odometer readings. Pepco's Pipeline Working Group recommended that an additional in-line inspection be conducted in 1997 using ultrasonic inspection tool technology.

1997 Pipetronix In-line Inspection. Pepco contracted with the ultrasonic in-line inspection contractor Pipetronix[21] to conduct a pipeline inspection on August 16, 1997. Before conducting its ultrasonic inspection tool survey, Pipetronix subcontracted for an in-line caliper tool[22] survey, which was completed on August 11, 1997. Pipetronix had the caliper tool run to confirm that there were no physical obstructions in the pipeline that would prevent passage of the ultrasonic inspection tool.

On August 16, 1997, Pipetronix examined the segment of the Piney Point Oil Pipeline from Ryceville to Chalk Point with an ultrasonic inspection tool. Pepco required that Pipetronix prepare a final report for the inspection that would include a complete, written survey report for the pipeline. The report would provide the pipeline operator data, including all types of corrosion, gouging, pipeline fittings (such as T-pieces,[23] valves, etc.), girth welds, wall thickness changes, special features (such as externally welded patches, insulating flanges, etc.), and differentiation between internal and external corrosion (for general surface corrosion, pitting, and channeling).[24]

According to the contract, Pipetronix was to use a multi-step process to identify and interpret each feature in the pipeline, as follows:

1. Field check of the data at random locations immediately after the tool run is completed,

2. Search of the data by automatic computer programs to detect girth welds, pipe installations, defects (internal and external), markers, and other features,

---

[21] On November 25, 1999, Pipeline Integrity International Ltd. acquired the Pipetronix Group. The subsidiary PII North America, Inc., now controls those assets that belonged to Pipetronix in the United States.

[22] A *caliper tool* is an in-line inspection device used to determine the geometrical condition of the pipe, including the size and location of abnormalities.

[23] A *T-piece* is normally a tee pipe-fitting welded into a pipeline, although alternatively, a T-piece may be made by welding a pipe stub to a pipeline and drilling a hole into the pipeline.

[24] National Association of Corrosion Engineers Standard RP0102-2002, *Recommended Practice In-Line Inspection of Pipelines*, table 1, lists the types of in-line inspection tools and inspection purposes.

3. Computer generation, with relevant input from the interpreter, of a features list,

4. Interpretation by the interpreter of each feature found in the search phase.

The completed pipeline features list was to contain all features recorded in the tool run and present the results of the interpretation in condensed form. The report noted that data collected during the tool run were systematically evaluated according to criteria defined in the contract between Pipetronix and Pepco. Pipetronix performed this evaluation in five phases:

- Phase 1: Handover of data from the workshop (integration within the management of the department, handover meeting, familiarizing of the project leader);

- Phase 2: Preparation of the interpretation;

- Phase 3: Main interpretation (automatic interpretation, manual interpretation, feature list editing, quality check);

- Phase 4: Summarizing of the results (handover of the features list to the client, discussion of the results for the final report, documenting of the features, completion of the final report, quality check);

- Phase 5: Project completion, including forwarding the final report to Pepco.

After the August 1997 Pipetronix inspection, the pipeline segment from Ryceville to Chalk Point was excavated and exposed in 12 places in fall 1997. The pipeline was inspected and repaired at locations indicated by the ultrasonic inspection to have the deepest and most severe corrosion. At these locations, Pepco determined that the Pipetronix in-line inspection data correlated relatively well with the field measurements made of the pipe-wall thickness using an ultrasonic testing instrument. However, Pepco found that some locations had more severe corrosion than had been indicated by the ultrasonic inspection.

Pipetronix provided the results of the inspection of the Ryceville to Chalk Point segment of pipeline to Pepco in a final report dated January 20, 1998. The final report included general information about the ultrasonic inspection tool used, the ultrasonic measuring method, the design of the tool, the benefits and limitations of the tool, the survey procedures, the procedures for evaluating the collected data, and a detailed table of pipeline features.

Pipetronix's interpretation of the tool data was included in an appendix to the final report entitled "Features List." The report identified and located by station number various pipeline features, including external metal loss, internal metal loss, laminations, flanges, field bends, weld-o-lets, hot bends, dents, sleeves, markers, girth welds, valves, and T-pieces. Pepco used Pipetronix's in-line inspection report to establish the baseline conditions of the pipeline and to conduct its excavation and field inspection program.

Excluding various aboveground features at the pig launcher and receiver, the Pipetronix features list identified three T-pieces in the pipeline. Two T-pieces were approximately 1,519 feet apart, one on each side of Swanson Creek, at odometer stations 51887.20 and 53406.10. The third identified T-piece, which was actually the buckle that failed on April 7, 2000, was identified as being located at odometer station 53526.55.

After conducting a postaccident review of the inspection log for the August 1997 in-line inspection, Pipetronix determined that its analyst had inaccurately interpreted the log indication at odometer station 53526.55 as a T-piece. At the time of the in-line inspection, Pipetronix's software reference library did not include a standard image of an outward protruding buckle, such as the one at odometer station 53526.55. Pipetronix acknowledged that, based on its knowledge at the time, the feature should have been interpreted as an "unknown."[25]

Before the April 7, 2000, accident, Pepco had authorized another ultrasonic pipeline inspection to be conducted by Pipetronix in April 2000. At the time of the accident, Pepco was cleaning the pipeline to prepare it for this upcoming in-line inspection to take place later in April 2000.

Operations

The pipeline was operated manually for startup and shutdown.[26] The Ryceville Station was normally left unattended after initial system startup when no pump was operating at Ryceville. Pipeline operating data were not periodically transmitted to the Piney Point Terminal. The pipeline monitoring system transmitted pipeline pressure, temperature, and flow rate alarms to Piney Point. The pipeline alarms were displayed on the computer screen at the Piney Point Terminal, and audible alarms alerted the ST Services operator on duty to pipeline operating conditions that were outside predetermined limits. Using his computer terminal, the ST Services shift supervisor's operating practice while serving as the pipeline controller was to verify the system alarm status, as well as pressure, temperature, and flow rate information, once each 8-hour shift. The alarm data were stored at each station for 30 days and could be printed locally at each station if a data review was desired. The pipeline computer monitoring system provided the operations data it was designed to gather during No. 6 fuel oil transfers.

Pepco's *Piney Point Oil Pipeline Manual* required that during a No. 6 fuel oil transfer, the ST Services pipeline controller had to conduct a daily recording of meter readings and to communicate daily with Pepco operations personnel to ascertain the delivered quantity, flow rate, available tank capacity, and estimated time of operation completion. The Pepco manual further required that the ST Services pipeline controller

---

[25] A postaccident Office of Pipeline Safety report that evaluated the 1997 Pipetronix survey found that the ultrasonic inspection tool provided good characterization of the pipeline's physical elements, such as the valves, tees, bends, fittings, and points of deformation. The report also found that the tool recorded an indication of a buckle at the location of odometer station 53526.55, but the Pipetronix analyst mischaracterized the indication as a T-piece.

[26] The pipeline was operated on an as-needed basis when a No. 6 fuel oil transfer was required for a generating station.

record the pipeline pressure, temperature, and flow rate at Piney Point at 4-hour intervals during a No. 6 fuel oil transfer.

The ST Services pipeline controller did not continuously monitor pipeline operating conditions. The ST Services pipeline controller could receive a call from the system that a pipeline operating parameter was out of allowable tolerance, and he could then access the monitoring system to determine the nature of the alarm.

Pipeline flushing was performed at the end of each No. 6 fuel oil transfer.[27] Piping alignments for pigging operations were set up similarly to a flushing operation, although there were obvious differences in routing the product through the pig traps. The product did not flow through the meter at the Chalk Point Station during a flushing operation or during the pigging operation on the day of the accident. In addition, the meters and pressure-sensing points at the Chalk Point Station were not in the oil flow path, and the temperature-sensing equipment was not in the direct oil flow path to the Ryceville Station. The pipeline monitoring system was not capable of monitoring pipeline operating conditions because of the meter location and the locations of the sensing points. Pipeline shift supervisors and operators had no predetermined line balance limits to follow to assess pumped and delivered product volumes during flushing or pigging operations. Pepco's *Piney Point Oil Pipeline Manual* did not require any pipeline operations personnel to perform periodic line balance calculations during a flushing or pigging operation, nor did they do so.

The abnormal operating condition procedures described in section 7.4, paragraph 5.2, of Pepco's *Piney Point Oil Pipeline Manual* required the ST Services terminal duty operator or pipeline operator mechanic to report any abnormal fuel oil system operating condition that was indicated by 1) an alarm condition on the pipeline monitoring system, 2) a visual indication of a local pressure or level indication, 3) an abnormal system operating indication from the Pepco generating station senior power plant operator, 4) or the One-Call system. Paragraph 5.3 provides an example of an abnormal system operating condition, which it termed an:

> Increase, decrease or an alarm differential in the fuel oil system pressure or flow rate outside of normal steady state operating conditions as indicated by a computer monitoring alarm condition or a local pressure instrumentation.

Pipeline Maps and Records

The original Piney Point Oil Pipeline alignment sheets and as-built drawings were destroyed in a fire before Pepco purchased the pipeline in 1976. Title 49 CFR 195.404 requires operators to have maps and records that include at least the following information: 1) the location and identification of breakout tanks, pump stations, scraper and sphere facilities, pipeline valves, cathodically protected facilities, facilities in an immediate response area not equipped to fail safe, facility rights-of-way, and overpressure safety devices; 2) all crossings of public roads, railroads, rivers, buried utilities, and

---

[27] *Flushing* is the process of pumping flushing oil in the reverse direction of normal flow in the pipeline to displace the No. 6 fuel oil from the pipeline before it cools to the point that it cannot be pumped.

foreign pipelines; 3) the maximum operating pressure of each pipeline; and 4) the diameter, grade, type, and nominal wall thickness of all pipe. During 1993 and 1994, Pepco had pipeline alignment maps made based on aerial photography and created drawings for aboveground piping of Piney Point Oil Pipeline facilities.

Meteorological Information

At mid-afternoon, on April 7, 2000, Reagan Washington National Airport (about 40 miles northwest of the accident scene) recorded a maximum wind speed of about 19 mph. The temperature was 77° F, and the sky was overcast. By mid-afternoon on April 8, 2000, wind gusts of about 50 mph were recorded at the airport. Conditions were rainy, and the temperature was approximately 57° F. During the evening of April 8, rains in excess of 1 inch and winds over 50 mph were experienced in the Chalk Point area.

Pepco Oil Spill Preparedness

Under 49 CFR 194.101, pipeline operators are required to submit a spill response plan to the Research and Special Programs Administration (RSPA) for review and approval. Pepco had provided such a plan to RSPA. According to the regulation, the plan must address a response to a worst-case discharge and the threat from such a discharge. It must also include procedures for conducting drills, including identifying the types of drills to be conducted and their schedules. Appendix A to Part 194 provides recommendations concerning the topics that the response plan must address. Under section 7, concerning drill procedures, it is recommended that drills be conducted on the following topics at the following frequencies:

- Quarterly drills on emergency procedures and notifications of qualified individuals for manned pipelines;

- Quarterly drills involving emergency actions by assigned operating or maintenance personnel and notifications of qualified individuals for unmanned pipelines;

- Annual tabletop exercises involving the shore-based management team;

- A drill once every 3 years that exercises the entire response plan for each response zone of the pipeline system.

In September 1996, a tabletop exercise was conducted at Chalk Point under the direction of RSPA's Office of Pipeline Safety, with the participation of the Coast Guard. The response exercise involved a hypothetical spill at the Pepco Morgantown facility of 800 barrels of No. 6 fuel oil into the Wicomico River. This was a coastal inland waterway release scenario, within the Coast Guard's jurisdiction. (The EPA did not participate in the drill.) The Office of Pipeline Safety sponsored the tabletop exercise to assess Pepco's pipeline emergency preparedness under the National Preparedness for Response Exercise

Program and the Oil Pollution Act of 1990. Specifically, the objectives of the tabletop exercise were to:

> Validate the emergency response plans and procedures of Pepco, and to enhance participants' knowledge of the appropriate plan and procedures (e.g. Facility Response Plan, Area Contingency Plan, State Contingency Plan, etc.)[28]

In the review that followed the exercise, Pepco received the following recommendations addressing incident management:

> The Pepco FRP [Facility Response Plan] should be revised to reflect how Pepco intends to direct response and resolve spill-related issues jointly with local, state, and federal responders. Additional training on the roles and responsibilities involved in these assignments should reinforce the policies of the oil spill contingency plan. The training should include all potential response groups if possible, to assist each group in clarifying its role in response operations and as a part of the unified system. The SMT [Spill Management Team] should ensure that other Pepco personnel potentially involved in response operations are also trained in their roles. New personnel assignment to perform the functions of the Incident Command System, revisions of their roles and responsibilities, and a description of how these will interact with the local, state and federal responders in the unified system should be reflected in the FRP.[29]

According to Pepco,[30] Revision No. 3 (dated March 13, 1997) of the *Oil Spill Emergency Response Plan for the Ryceville Pumping Station and Pipeline* incorporated the above comments. On August 26, 1997, Pepco submitted Revision No. 3 of the plan to the Office of Pipeline Safety, which, on October 27, 1997, completed review of the revised plan. The Office of Pipeline Safety stated that the revised plan adequately addressed the response planning recommendations made by the Office of Pipeline Safety based on the drill results.

Between January 1999 and April 7, 2000, at least five notification drills were conducted for the Piney Point Oil Pipeline. Equipment deployment drills were conducted in July and November 1999.

Postaccident Actions

Office of Pipeline Safety Postaccident Requirements

An April 12, 2000, Office of Pipeline Safety corrective action order stated that Pepco must not operate the Piney Point Oil Pipeline until the company:

---

[28] *Pepco Spill Management Team Tabletop Exercise Report,* September 1996, prepared by the Corporate Response Group, Inc., for RSPA's Office of Pipeline Safety.

[29] *Pepco Spill Management Team Tabletop Exercise Report.*

[30] *Summary of Changes: Ryceville Facility Response Plan* –Revision 3a, dated May 4, 1998.

1. Develops adequate repair procedures,

2. Reviews and addresses procedures for leak detection,

3. Develops a plan with corrective measures to address leak factors including:

    •Review existing instrumentation and improve manual line balance,

    •Develop and implement a training program for operations personnel,

    •Provide specific procedures and training for pipeline-system monitoring,

    •Review qualifications of operations personnel, and

    •Provide classroom and practical training exercises for the above training items.

In an amended corrective action order issued on May 4, 2000, the Office of Pipeline Safety further required Pepco to:

1. [Conduct] Hydrostatic test[s] for integrity of pipe segment from Swanson Creek to Chalk Point,

2. Review previous internal inspection, make needed repairs, and plan future inspections,

3. Implement operations procedures for line monitoring during pigging activities,

4. Review and update schematic drawings.

Pipeline Safety Actions Since Accident

Since the accident, Pepco began and Mirant continued (after its purchase of the Piney Point Oil Pipeline) to make improvements to comply with, and in some cases exceed, the Office of Pipeline Safety's corrective action orders. Mirant prepared an integrity study to assess the risks posed by pipe wrinkles,[31] to establish acceptance criteria for pipe wrinkles, and to remove all those wrinkles or defects not satisfying the acceptance criteria. Mirant also developed additional pipeline repair procedures. After all inspections and replacements were completed, the entire pipeline system was hydrostatically tested. The transport temperature for No. 6 fuel oil was reduced temporarily from 160° F to 125° F until the influence of heat on pipeline movement could be studied.

Mirant installed supervisory control and data acquisition (SCADA) systems[32] with software-based leak detection and radar tank gauges with remote reading capability on all Piney Point Oil Pipeline tanks, and the entire set of operations and maintenance procedures was rewritten. In support of this pipeline integrity focus, two different smart

---

[31] A *wrinkle* is a smooth wave deflection of the pipe wall and may have a single inward or outward deflection or may include a sinusoidal waveform with both inward and outward displacements.

[32] Pipeline controllers use SCADA systems to remotely monitor and control movement through pipelines. With a SCADA system, controllers can monitor flow rates and pressures along the lines and control valves and pumps to adjust the flow at pump stations and locations throughout the pipeline system.

pig technologies (ultrasonic and deformation inertial) were employed to inspect the entire pipeline system in May 2001. Mirant indicated that the evaluations were intended to provide a substantial new baseline for maintaining pipeline integrity, in addition to restoring pipeline activities.

Mirant has put in place a new diversified pipeline management team that has indicated it intends to continue to use industry-recognized pipeline consultants. This team intends to prepare and manage a long-term integrity plan for the pipeline, consistent with the integrity management rule in Federal pipeline safety regulations. Mirant has employed its own pipeline operating personnel, which, Mirant states, have been trained in the new procedures and equipment. Mirant has implemented an internal audit process that it says will provide further assurance that all current regulatory and industry best practices are maintained.

In accordance with the requirements at 49 CFR 194.101, Mirant submitted to RSPA in December 2001 a spill response plan dated May 2001. RSPA approved the plan on April 30, 2002. Mirant developed its facility emergency spill response plans with the assistance of industry experts. During the first 6 months of 2001, three revisions were made to the *Oil Spill Emergency Response Plan for the Ryceville Pumping Station and Pipeline*. Specifically, these changes addressed ownership and nomenclature adjustments, as well as additional revisions intended to clarify and simplify the plan. On July 27, 2001, Mirant published *Response Strategies for Southern Maryland.* Based on "operational experience gained during the Swanson Creek oil spill response and studies," the manual was intended to provide tactical response information for use as a pre-planning document for response managers and crews. The manual identified key control points along and off the pipeline corridor where response actions might be taken should a release occur. One of the main elements in the manual was a site summary sheet for each of the primary control point locations. The summary sheets were prepared with map and chart references with global positioning system location data, location and general access instructions, general release/flow paths, information concerning receiving water bodies and selected sensitive features, and response protocols and tactics. Shortly after the manual was published, Mirant personnel met with the members of the Local Emergency Planning Committee, which represents the local public response agencies of the four surrounding counties, to familiarize them with the implementation of the manual.

In 2001, Mirant conducted 11 drills concerning spill response (2 deployment drills, 5 tabletop drills, and 4 qualified individual notification drills). As of June 1, 2002, Mirant had conducted four spill response drills (one deployment, one tabletop, and two qualified individual notification) in 2002.

Other Information

Incident Command System

The Incident Command System concept was developed as a consequence of fires that destroyed significant environmental assets in 1970 in Southern California. Agencies recognized that they needed a system that allowed them to work together effectively and efficiently when conducting responses to the broadest range of emergencies, including incidents involving threats to lives, property, and the environment. A multi-agency task force subsequently developed the Incident Command System.

The system consists of procedures for controlling personnel, facilities, equipment, and communications during an incident response. It is designed to be used from the time an incident occurs until response operations are completed. The Incident Command System structure has five major functional areas—command, operations, planning, logistics, and finance—but the structure is flexible and can be accommodated to the specific needs of each response. Consequently, it can be used for any type or size of incident. It provides a framework under which agencies may communicate and function using uniform terminology and operating procedures.

The system is widely used by Federal, State, and local responders. Since the development of the Incident Command System concept, Incident Command System structures have been used at hundreds of incidents with general success. In February 1996, the Coast Guard officially adopted the National Interagency Incident Management System Incident Command System and has developed various training modules for it.

In an April 24, 2001, letter to the Safety Board, the EPA Federal On-Scene Coordinator for the Chalk Point accident stated that:

> EPA currently has no formal policy on the use of Incident Command System/Unified Command. The National Response Team's Technical Assistance document has been distributed to all EPA on-scene coordinator[s], and EPA headquarters has encouraged the inclusion of the Incident Command System/Unified Command into their Area Contingency Plans (ACP). However, EPA's Regions have been provided the flexibility, consistent with the National Response Team's Technical Assistance Document, to adopt response management structures that use an Incident Command System that may be consistent with National Interagency Incident Management System [NIIMS]. The Region III Inland Area Contingency Plan calls for a Unified Incident Command System that is not based on NIIMS.

EPA has provided no written guidance to its regions on the use of Incident Command System/Unified Command beyond that provided in the National Response Team Technical Assistance Document *Incident Command System/Unified Command— Managing Responses to Oil Discharges and Hazardous Substance Releases under the National Contingency Plan*. The National Response Team, with the Regional Response Teams, constitutes the Federal component of the National Response System. The National Response Team and Regional Response Teams are made up of 16 Federal departments and agencies. The EPA chairs the National Response Team, and the Coast Guard serves as Vice Chair.

The EPA's Office of Emergency and Remedial Response is developing an EPA policy position on the Incident Command System.

Postaccident Assessments of Chalk Point Response

EPA Federal On-Scene Coordinator. In her postaccident report on the Chalk Point response,[33] the EPA Federal On-Scene Coordinator made numerous findings concerning a wide range of areas in which the response could have been improved and made suggestions to improve future responses. She acknowledged that the lack of a National Interagency Incident Management System-based Incident Command System structure hindered the establishment of resource tracking and accountability as the Chalk Point incident progressed. She also stated that because local responders were not included in the immediate response, their capabilities were not effectively used to disseminate information to the community or to coordinate response efforts.

Regional Response Team. In its April 5, 2001, report on the Chalk Point accident response,[34] the Regional Response Team review committee found that there appeared to have been no effective response management system, especially early in the incident. The committee considered that the task-oriented management structure originally used was not conducive to managing the rapid expansion of a major oil spill. The committee added that, although each incident is different, major oil spills have predictable elements that can be managed more effectively via Incident Command/Unified Command systems. As a result, the Regional Response Team review committee recommended that, in future incidents, the Incident Command/Unified Command system be immediately activated at the spill site to ensure that authority and responsibility are clearly assigned. Further, the Regional Response Team stated that the EPA should develop a guidance document on how to set up and run Incident Command/Unified Command systems, train all Federal On-Scene Coordinators in Incident Command/Unified Command systems, and consider augmenting the Federal On-Scene Coordinator with an Incident Command System/Unified Command management team.

Coast Guard. In his August 25, 2001, letter addressing lessons learned from the Chalk Point accident response, the Chief of Marine Safety for the Fifth Coast Guard District indicated that the significant delay in establishing an Incident Command System contributed to a fragmented and ineffective response. He further stated:

> The Coast Guard has adopted the Incident Command System (ICS) as its emergency response process. We have found ICS to be a very effective spill management tool; particularly as the system is used by most State and Local response entities as well.

---

[33] Environmental Protection Agency, *After-Action Report for Emergency Response at the Swanson Creek Oil Spill Site, Aquasco, Maryland, Prince George's, Charles, Calvert, and St. Mary's Counties 7 April 2000 to 16 May 2000.*

[34] *Swanson Preparedness and Response Review: Swanson Creek Marsh Oil Spill – April 2000*, Final Report, dated April 5, 2001.

He noted that, although it appeared that the oil was well-contained in the wetlands early in the response, other factors were at play (wind, predicted storm, etc.) that might have led experienced response managers to recognize the precarious nature of the situation. He indicated that responders conducting overflights or other assessment activities should have analyzed the gathered information more accurately and realized that the oil was liable to break out of containment and enter the Patuxent River.

He further found that the limited involvement of the local response community had a negative effect on the response effort. He indicated that local responders play a major role in site safety, provide local information needed by responders from other areas, and can help to establish the Unified Command and Incident Command System structures as soon as they arrive on the scene.

November 2000 Safety Board Hearing on Pipeline Safety

On November 15 and 16, 2000, the Safety Board held a pipeline safety hearing that focused on pipeline inspection, integrity verification, and leak detection and response. Participating in the meeting were representatives of Federal agencies, including the Safety Board, RSPA, and the Office of Pipeline Safety; the pipeline industry, including pipeline operators, in-line pipeline inspection services, and integrity assessment consultants; and academia and research institutes.[35]

In addition to addressing a wide range of other pipeline safety issues, pipeline industry representatives stressed the need for pipeline leak detection systems to have accurate pipeline instrumentation located at sensing sites. During the hearing, the RSPA Administrator stated that, to increase their efficiency, leak detection systems must be less dependent on the human pipeline controller. Hearing testimony also indicated that many leaks could be detected in a matter of minutes with a computational pipeline monitoring system, which would reduce the reliance of pipeline system operating parameters on human input.

---

[35] For additional information on the presentations made during the November 2000 pipeline safety hearing, see the Web link at <http://www.ntsb.gov/events/2000/pipeline_hearing/default.htm>.

Analysis

The Accident

About 0715 on April 7, 2000, employees of Pepco's contractor, ST Services, launched a cleaning pig in flushing oil from Pepco's Chalk Point Station toward Ryceville Station on the Piney Point Oil Pipeline. For the next several hours, periodic tank levels were taken for the Chalk Point (origin) and the Ryceville (destination) Stations' flushing oil tanks, but tank volumes were not calculated from the tank level readings and evaluated for line balance as the pumping operation proceeded. Because the pumping was progressing faster than expected, ST Services personnel operating the pipeline expected the cleaning pig to arrive at the Ryceville Station between about 1300 and 1330, but it did not. The ST Services Chalk Point operator became concerned and double-checked the tank level about 1412 because the pig had not arrived at Ryceville, and the Chalk Point pump began cavitating at 1430. About the same time, the flow of oil stopped at the Ryceville Station.

By 1440, pipeline personnel had initiated the acquisition of current tank level measurements for line balance calculations at both stations and the checking of the Chalk Point manifold for misaligned valves. By 1534, they had calculated that Ryceville had not received 3,089 barrels (129,738 gallons) of the oil that had been pumped from Chalk Point. At 1538, pipeline operating personnel shut down the pipeline and initiated surface inspections at locations where the pipeline crosses roads and Swanson Creek to look for an oil leak. By 1802, a pipeline aerial patrol, which had been launched earlier at the direction of the Pepco Chalk Point general supervisor for operations, had reported sighting a pipeline leak in the wetlands near Swanson Creek, not far from the Chalk Point Station.

Postaccident calculations performed by the Piney Point Oil Pipeline owners, which were based on review of the recorded pipeline pressure information, the operating conditions at the time of the accident, the size of the crack, and the amount of product spilled, indicated that the pipe failure occurred before 0930 on April 7, 2000, probably when the Chalk Point pump was started, about 0715, and the pipeline pressure was at its highest level. The Safety Board reviewed this analysis and found it credible.

The pipeline ruptured at a wrinkle in a section of pipe that had been field-bent during initial construction of the pipeline in 1971 and 1972. The deformation, or wrinkle, that failed was a single outward deflection of the pipe wall, commonly described as a buckle. After the pipeline was placed in service, forces imposed on the deformed area of the bend, including the normal operating pressure and thermal cycles in the pipeline, caused repeated straining and eventual cracking until the pipe at the deformed area failed.

Pipeline In-line Inspection

Although in-line inspections were not mandated, Pepco maintained a program under which it periodically had in-line inspections conducted on the Piney Point Oil Pipeline to help ensure pipeline integrity. Pipetronix, an ultrasonic in-line inspection contractor, had conducted the last inspection of the pipeline before the accident on August 16, 1997. When the April 7, 2000, accident occurred, Pepco was preparing the Piney Point Oil Pipeline for another in-line inspection.

In accordance with its contract with Pepco for the August 1997 in-line inspection, Pipetronix examined the segment of the Piney Point Oil Pipeline from Ryceville to Chalk Point to identify corrosion, gouging, pipeline fittings, girth welds, wall thickness changes, special features, and differentiation between internal and external corrosion. Pipetronix interpreted and checked the ultrasonic tool data from the inspection using computer-based systems and manual review by its technicians. The Pipetronix report to Pepco concerning the in-line inspection results and Pipetronix's interpretation of the results included an appendix that identified and located various pipeline features by station number.

Pipetronix's interpretation of the ultrasonic tool data contained a significant inaccuracy for the feature at odometer station 53526.55. This feature, which was found after the accident to be a buckle but was inaccurately interpreted by the Pipetronix analyst as a T-piece, failed and resulted in the leak on April 7, 2000. Based on interpretation of the data available to Pipetronix at the time of the inspection, the Pipetronix analyst should have interpreted the feature as an "unknown" because it did not match the signal characteristic for a T-piece. Had Pepco been notified that the feature was an unknown, it might have attempted to determine the feature's true characteristics, through excavation or other means. Therefore, the Safety Board concludes that because Pipetronix incorrectly interpreted the results of its ultrasonic tool data for the pipeline feature at odometer station 53526.55, Pepco was not alerted to the need for additional evaluation of the pipe at the location where it subsequently ruptured. After the accident, Pipetronix updated its reference library and training materials to include the signal characteristics of the outward protruding buckle that failed in this accident.

Evaluation of Pipe Wrinkles

After the accident, RSPA required Mirant (which became the pipeline's owner some months after the accident) to prepare an integrity study of the Piney Point Oil Pipeline before it would allow the pipeline to be returned to service. Data from the 1997 in-line inspection of the pipeline were compared to the actual geometry of various wrinkles in pipeline bends, obtained after excavating the most severe wrinkles and determining the geometry by field measurements. After correlation between the in-line inspection data and the field measurements was completed, the 1997 in-line inspection data were used as the basis for the evaluation of wrinkles that had not been excavated and inspected. An analysis was performed to determine if identified wrinkles needed to be removed. As a result of this work, Mirant developed quantitative acceptance criteria for pipe wrinkles remaining in the pipeline. RSPA accepted the analysis that indicated that some wrinkles could remain in the pipeline, and RSPA allowed the pipeline to return to service.

Field bends containing wrinkles were installed in pipelines before the hazardous liquid pipeline safety regulations went into effect in 1970. Since then, pipeline regulations have prohibited the installation of pipe containing wrinkle bends during pipeline construction.[36] However, pipe wrinkles that were not discovered during the construction inspection process or that formed sometime after construction are still periodically found in pipelines.

According to RSPA's pipeline integrity management rule, when an in-line inspection tool is selected by a pipeline operator to assess the condition of the pipeline, it must be "capable of detecting corrosion and deformation anomalies including dents, gouges, and grooves" in high-consequence areas.[37] The regulation states that "an operator must evaluate all anomalies and repair those anomalies that could reduce a pipeline's integrity."[38] Although the language in this regulation does not specifically designate wrinkles as a category of deformation anomaly, when questioned by Safety Board staff, RSPA officials indicated that the regulation applies to wrinkles.

Wrinkles can sometimes be identified through the use of in-line inspection tools. However, operators do not have nationally recognized quantitative criteria with which to assess the effect of a specific wrinkle characteristic on a pipe or to determine whether a pipeline can be safely operated while it contains some wrinkles. Therefore, the Safety Board concludes that because pipeline operators have no nationally recognized criteria with which to evaluate pipe wrinkles, they may not be effectively determining whether pipe containing wrinkles should be allowed to remain in service. The Safety Board believes that RSPA should establish quantitative criteria, based on engineering evaluations, for determining whether a wrinkle may be allowed to remain in a pipeline.

Leak Detection

After the Chalk Point leak began, sometime before 0930 on April 7, 2000, it was hours before those operating the Piney Point Oil Pipeline recognized that a line balance shortage, which might indicate a leak, was developing. The leak might have been recognized much sooner if more systematic leak detection procedures and practices had been in place and used.

During normal deliveries of No. 6 fuel oil to the Chalk Point Generating Station, Pepco's automated pipeline monitoring system was designed to provide alarms for pressure, temperature, and flow rate to the pipeline controller for operating conditions

---

[36] 49 CFR 195.212.

[37] 49 CFR 195.452(c)(1)(i)(A).

[38] 49 CFR 195.452(h)(1).

outside of predetermined limits. During the pigging operation on the day of the accident, however, the meters and pressure-sensing points at Chalk Point were not in the flushing oil's flow path, and the temperature-sensing equipment was not in the direct flow path to Ryceville. Thus, Pepco's automated pipeline monitoring and leak detection system on the Piney Point Oil Pipeline did not alert the ST Services personnel to the developing problem.

With respect to manual monitoring of the pipeline, ST Services did not require its personnel to perform line balance calculations while conducting either normal pipeline or pigging operations, nor did the procedures in Pepco's *Piney Point Oil Pipeline Manual* include such requirements. Although ST Services personnel took tank level measurements at both the Chalk Point and Ryceville Stations throughout the morning of April 7, they did not use this information to evaluate whether product had been lost from the pipeline. Based on the speed of the pigging operation and his previous experience, the ST Services Chalk Point operator updated the estimated cleaning pig arrival time at the Ryceville Station from about 1415 to between 1300 and 1330. Even when the pig failed to arrive during this period, ST Services personnel still did not evaluate the tank level information to check the line balance. It was not until the Chalk Point pump began cavitating and the flow of oil stopped at the Ryceville Station, about 1430, that ST Services personnel recognized a problem. Between 1440 and 1534, using tank level measurements for line balance calculations, they determined that Ryceville had not received 3,089 barrels of the oil that had been pumped from Chalk Point, and they shut the pipeline down at 1538.

On April 7, 2000, therefore, Pepco's procedures, as provided in the *Piney Point Oil Pipeline Manual*, were inadequate because they did not require ST Services personnel to conduct line balancing during pigging operations, and ST Services' practices were inadequate because they did not include effective line balancing during the pigging operation. Although some manual tank levels were obtained throughout the day, they were not evaluated. Had line balance been determined on a timely basis, the line balance discrepancy would likely have been discovered within about an hour of its occurrence. The Safety Board concludes that the absence of effective pipeline monitoring procedures and practices, including periodic line balancing, delayed the discovery of the fuel oil shortage on April 7, 2000, which delayed the pipeline shutdown and allowed more oil to leak from the pipeline.

As a result of a pipeline accident in North Blenheim, New York,[39] the Safety Board issued Safety Recommendation P-91-1 to RSPA. It read:

---

[39] National Transportation Safety Board, *Liquid Propane Pipeline Rupture and Fire, Texas Eastern Products Pipeline Company, North Blenheim, New York, March 13, 1990*, Pipeline Accident Report NTSB/PAR-91/01 (Washington, DC: NTSB, 1991).

P-91-1

Define the operating parameters that must be monitored by pipeline operators to detect abnormal operations and establish performance standards that must be met by pipeline monitoring systems installed to detect and locate leaks.

Safety Recommendation P-91-1 is classified "Open—Unacceptable Response."

RSPA, in its 1991 and 1992 responses to the recommendation, indicated that it intended to conduct a study of SCADA systems. In response to a 1997 follow-up status inquiry from the Safety Board, RSPA indicated that it would soon issue rulemaking concerning leak detection standards.

In 1998, RSPA incorporated parts of an industry standard for leak detection, API Standard 1130, *Computational Pipeline Monitoring*, in its hazardous liquid pipeline safety regulations. In 49 CFR Part 195, computational pipeline monitoring is defined as a "software-based monitoring tool that alerts the pipeline dispatcher of a possible pipeline operating anomaly that may be indicative of a commodity release." Title 49 CFR 195.134, which is the safety regulation requiring the use of API Standard 1130 for design, applies when operators are replacing a component of an existing computational pipeline monitoring system or installing a new computational pipeline monitoring system on a pipeline; the regulation does not require that such systems be installed.

Since the April 2000 accident, Pepco initiated, and Mirant completed, the installation of a new SCADA system that meets API Standard 1130, and a pipeline controller will continuously monitor it. This system includes additional instrumentation, sensors, and controls, as well as a computer model that uses current pipeline operating conditions. The system continuously calculates line balances to enable early detection and warning, and it allows the pipeline controller to initiate remote shutdown. Mirant now operates the pipeline with its own employees, and the pipeline controller is engaged in active analysis and monitoring of pipeline operations. Mirant has revised the operating procedures so that the pipeline controller initiates an immediate shutdown when a flow shortage outside of predetermined limits is indicated by its new SCADA-based leak detection system.

At a Safety Board pipeline safety hearing held in November 2000, panelists discussed various types of automated monitoring systems that make leak detection possible within a matter of minutes. In contrast, manual line balancing relies on acquisition of data by pipeline operators. Manual computation and evaluation are then required to develop the pipeline operating data. The manual process requires more time to complete than an automated system, and the input data are more susceptible to human error than data obtained and used by an automated monitoring system.

On December 1, 2000, RSPA issued a new regulation at 49 CFR 195.452, requiring hazardous liquid operators with 500 or more miles of pipeline to provide pipeline integrity management. On January 16, 2002, RSPA amended the regulation to include operators that own or operate less than 500 miles of regulated hazardous liquid pipelines. The regulation requires that operators have a "means to detect" leaks on their pipeline systems in high-consequence areas, but it does not specify what constitutes adequate means to detect leaks.

RSPA officials met with Safety Board staff on May 16, 2002. In response to Safety Board staff questions about how RSPA will enforce the new leak detection requirements, RSPA officials indicated that they are developing specific criteria for defining adequate leak detection measures and that the criteria will be posted and enforced.[40] The Safety Board supports this effort and encourages RSPA to expedite the development of the criteria and, as part of the process, to consider increased system automation to ensure timely leak detection.

Leak-related Notifications

Once the ST Services pipeline operators confirmed that they had a leak, they began to initiate an emergency response. The emergency response was affected by several communications breakdowns. Pepco did not provide accurate information about the volume of the Chalk Point oil release to public agencies, nor did Pepco ensure that its internal information exchanges were effectively coordinated. The failures left responders with inadequate information with which to evaluate the threat posed by the release.

In the case of the Chalk Point accident, the response of deploying booms initially contained the oil spill, despite failures to effectively notify responders about the scope of the accident and to inform local response agencies early in the response effort. However, in future incidents involving pipeline leaks, such notification errors could cause responders to fail to respond with the resources needed to deal with a release, which could have negative consequences.

Inaccurate National Response Center Notification

Between 1538, when the pipeline was shut down, and 1850, when the National Response Center received notification of the Chalk Point spill, miscommunications and the creation of a release estimate lacking any factual basis took place among the various Pepco officials managing the release. By the time they shut down the pipeline, ST Services personnel were aware that they had a line balance discrepancy of about 3,000 barrels (126,000 gallons). Sometime before 1620, the ST Services assistant terminal manager told the Pepco engineering supervisor that the line balance discrepancy was about 3,000 barrels. The Pepco engineering supervisor informed the Pepco Chalk Point general supervisor for operations about the discrepancy at 1620, stating that it was about 2,000 to 3,000 barrels. At this time, the Pepco Chalk Point general supervisor for operations noted in his log that there was a discrepancy of 2,000 barrels.

---

[40] In addition, RSPA is soliciting research proposals to advance leak detection technologies by improving leak detection timeliness and accuracy and by developing improved means of detecting small pipeline leaks.

About 1827, a still more significant error took place concerning the estimation of the size of the spill. The Pepco Chalk Point shift supervisor told the Pepco qualified individual (when pressed to provide an estimate) that the amount of the spill was "1,000 gallons, 2,000 gallons, [expletive] mess, tell them what you want." This unfounded estimate was reported to the Pepco Chalk Point general supervisor for operations, who, in consultation with the Pepco senior environmental coordinator during a phone conversation, agreed to report a release of 2,000 gallons to the National Response Center and the Maryland Department of the Environment. About 1840, ST Services provided additional confirmation to the Pepco Chalk Point general supervisor that the line balance shortage was approximately 3,000 barrels (126,000 gallons). About 1850, the Pepco senior environmental coordinator called the National Response Center and reported a 2,000-gallon No. 2 fuel oil release from a pipeline at Pepco's Chalk Point Generating Station, even though the Pepco Chalk Point general supervisor had updated information that the line balance shortage was actually about 3,000 barrels (126,000 gallons).

By 2015, the estimated release amount of 3,000 barrels (126,000 gallons) had been posted on the Chalk Point command center information blackboard. Shortly after 2100, the Pepco engineering group confirmed with line balance calculations that the amount of flushing oil involved in the release was 3,089 barrels (129,738 gallons).

Pepco officials could have updated the National Response Center when they learned that the information they had initially reported was inaccurate, but they did not. The Pepco senior environmental coordinator learned within 2 hours that the 2,000-gallon release estimate he had given the National Response Center did not approach the true magnitude of the release, but neither he nor any other Pepco manager updated the report. When asked why he never updated the National Response Center, the Pepco senior environmental coordinator said he believed that by 2130 on April 7, representatives of all the notified agencies were on the scene or were in contact with each other. In fact, the EPA Federal On-Scene Coordinator was not advised of the revised spill estimate until she arrived at Chalk Point at 1015 on April 8, about 13 hours after Pepco had confirmation that the likely size of the spill was 3,089 barrels (129,738 gallons). Thus, those oil spill responders who received notification from the National Response Center were not informed of the significant size of the product release and the spill's potential impact on the environment until they arrived on the scene.

During the May 16, 2002, meeting between RSPA officials and Safety Board staff, RSPA officials stated that National Response Center notification reports are intended to provide responders, as quickly as possible, the information they need to activate appropriate resources to control, mitigate, and/or clean up a product spill. Emergency responders, as well as accident investigators, rely on the information provided by the National Response Center when preparing their response efforts. Inaccurate or incomplete information can hamper these activities. For instance, if the initial information reported erroneously indicates that the release is minor, some Government responders needed on the scene to carry out containment or mitigation efforts may decide not to respond to the accident. And if they do respond, they may not bring sufficient resources to manage the spill. For those Government agencies that send personnel to the accident, the National

Response Center report may be the only information that the responders have before arriving on the scene. The more complete the information is, the better prepared Government responders will be to react to the particular circumstances of the accident.

In addition to the Chalk Point accident, the Safety Board is aware of other cases in which pipeline owners or operators reporting an incident to the National Response Center did not update their initial reports when more comprehensive and accurate information became available.[41] The Safety Board concludes that because pipeline owners and operators sometimes do not update their initial reports to the National Response Center, the notifications provided to emergency responders may not always contain the complete and accurate information needed to develop an effective incident response. Therefore, the Safety Board believes that RSPA should require pipeline owners and operators to provide follow-up telephone updates to the National Response Center when they discover that the information they initially reported contains significant errors or when they identify significant new information directly related to the reporting criteria.

Limited Involvement of Local Response Agencies

Pepco considered that, under the Chalk Point oil spill response plan, the release did not meet the criteria for notification of local response agencies, which were "fire, explosion, personal injury or release or significant threat of release off-site." Although the accident might not have immediately met these specific criteria, Pepco should have realized that the Chalk Point leak, due to its proximity to Swanson Creek, which fed into the Patuxent River, had the potential for a significant off-site release. However, Pepco did not contact local response agencies, including the Prince George's County Fire Department. As a result, the resources of the local response agencies were not utilized as soon as possible.

In her postaccident review, the EPA Federal On-Scene Coordinator stated that she believed the exclusion of local responders from the initial response (having been notified only once State responders were already on-scene) had a negative impact on the response operations, particularly with respect to the dissemination of information to the community and the ability to coordinate response efforts. In addition, the Chief of Marine Safety for the Fifth Coast Guard District stated, in an August 25, 2000, letter addressing lessons learned from the Chalk Point accident, that the local responders are needed to ensure the safety of the site, share local knowledge with the spill management team, and mobilize essential resources to the scene.

Mirant, the current owner of the Piney Point Oil Pipeline, has significantly revised the oil spill response procedures for the pipeline. In April 2002, RSPA approved Mirant's oil spill response plan. After the Chalk Point accident, the *Oil Spill Emergency Response Plan for the Ryceville Pumping Station and Pipeline* was revised to improve and clarify it.

---

[41] A March 30, 1998, accident in Sandy Springs, Georgia, that was originally reported to the National Response Center as a release of 150 gallons of gasoline was later found to be a release of over 15,800 gallons. An August 20, 2001, accident in Jackson County, Oklahoma, that was initially reported to the National Response Center as a release of 8,400 gallons of crude oil was later found to be a release of about 126,000 gallons.

Further, on July 27, 2001, Mirant published the manual *Response Strategies for Southern Maryland*, which was based on "operational experience gained during the Swanson Creek oil spill response and studies."[42] The Safety Board notes that Mirant personnel met with the members of the Local Emergency Planning Committee, which represents the local public response agencies of the four surrounding counties, to familiarize the members with the implementation of the manual. In the less than 2 years since Mirant became the owner of the pipeline, it has conducted at least 15 drills concerning elements of effective spill response, and some of the drills have involved local response agencies. The Safety Board notes these Mirant efforts to provide prompt involvement of local response agencies in any future emergencies.

Incident Command

The Safety Board found that the lack of effective incident command had a negative effect on the emergency response to the Chalk Point release. ST Services, Pepco, and spill recovery contractors on the scene on April 7 and 8, 2000, were initially successful in deploying a boom system that contained the leading edge of the spill. On the night of April 8, however, with the arrival of a severe storm that included heavy rains and 50-mph winds, the boom containment system was overwhelmed. The spill escaped containment and ultimately traveled an estimated 17 miles (linear) downstream and oiled 40 miles of shoreline in Prince George's, Charles, Calvert, and St. Mary's Counties. Responders were unable to effectively mitigate the environmental impact of the oil's entry into the Patuxent River, due in part to incident management and oversight deficiencies.

The EPA Federal On-Scene Coordinator arrived on the scene at 1015 on April 8 and began attempting to coordinate the Unified Command without establishing an Incident Command System. Instead, she relied on a project management structure that gave the responsible party, Pepco, primary responsibility for directing and monitoring the activities of response contractors. Throughout April 8, the Unified Command's efforts were focused on containing the spill within the Swanson Creek wetlands area. Pepco's contractors conducted the booming operation based on the directions they received from Pepco officials, who received their orders from the Unified Command.

Management problems were evident even at this early stage. The Pepco officials working with the contractors were on rotating 8-hour shifts, and those personnel going off-duty sometimes did not fully discuss response developments and necessary tasks with those coming on-duty. This lack of continuity caused problems with task and status communication and coordination. Instances of miscommunication and problems with unclear lines of authority occurred. Important meetings were not attended by all necessary personnel, and Pepco contractors sometimes did not fully understand the tasks they were

---

[42] The manual is intended to provide tactical information for use as a pre-planning document for response managers and crews. It identifies key control points along and off the pipeline corridor where response actions may be taken should a release occur. The manual also includes a summary sheet for each of the primary control point locations.

assigned. The EPA Federal On-Scene Coordinator also did not have extensive Federal response resources to draw upon at this time.

A storm was predicted for that evening, and the Unified Command and the EPA Federal On-Scene Coordinator ordered, and Pepco's contractors took, reasonable precautions to maintain the containment they had achieved in the Swanson Creek wetlands area. However, the storm was more severe than had been anticipated, and the outer booms at the Patuxent River were breached about 2030, releasing a significant amount of oil into the river.

For the next 2 days (April 9 and 10), the Unified Command, under the direction of the EPA Federal On-Scene Coordinator, attempted to mount an effective response to the oil spill's escape into the river. Significant resource and organizational problems arose immediately. Pepco had difficulty obtaining contractor resources that could carry out marine operations, and the EPA Federal On-Scene Coordinator encountered similar problems when she attempted to augment the response effort with Federal resources. Even more importantly, the contractors hired by Pepco were not completing urgent assigned tasks, and the delays in the response effort were not being promptly and accurately reported to the Unified Command. The EPA Federal On-Scene Coordinator stated that in the 2 days following the escape of the oil into the river, the Unified Command repeatedly directed Pepco to ensure that several environmentally sensitive creeks leading into the river were protectively boomed. According to the EPA Federal On-scene Coordinator, Pepco repeatedly indicated that appropriate action was being taken and that the booms would be placed as soon as possible. As of April 11, no booms had been deployed to protect the creeks, and two creeks showed evidence of oil contamination.

To address the coordination and communication problems and the contractors' inability to complete assigned tasks, the EPA Federal On-Scene Coordinator decided that an Incident Command System structure had to be implemented. Such a system is designed to provide more direct Federal control over response activities, a quicker response to spill developments, greater access to a wider range of resources, and better responder coordination. Consequently, she requested at 1430 on April 10 that Coast Guard officials assisting on scene develop such a structure. She also urged Pepco to hire a spill management contractor to improve the logistics of its contractors' efforts.

On the morning of April 11, the Coast Guard Captain of the Port of Baltimore arrived with additional personnel to staff the Incident Command System structure that had been developed. The new personnel were deployed to monitor the field operations being conducted by Pepco's contractors to ensure that work was completed as directed. Almost immediately, with the marshalling of the additional personnel and equipment, the effectiveness of the recovery operations improved. Protective booms were provided for the threatened creeks on April 12 and 13. Within days, marine-specialist responders finished collecting the free oil in the main body of the Patuxent River, and they were able to concentrate their efforts on oil collection from the affected creeks and other environmental mediation projects.

In their postaccident assessments of the Chalk Point accident, both the Coast Guard and the Regional Response Team review committee concluded that the response would have benefited from earlier use of an Incident Command System as the incident's coordination and management structure. In fact, the Regional Response Team review committee recommended that the EPA develop a manual on how to use Incident Command System/Unified Command structures and train all Federal On-Scene Coordinators in Incident Command System/Unified Command principles. In her own assessment of the response, the EPA Federal On-Scene Coordinator acknowledged that the decision not to implement an Incident Command System structure immediately upon her arrival at the accident scene ultimately had a detrimental effect on the response effort.

Once the oil escaped from containment in the wetlands and the situation became more complex and difficult to resolve, the short-term project management approach could not achieve results with the speed and efficiency needed to avoid a serious environmental impact. The Incident Command System has proven its effectiveness in incidents covering a wide range of transportation modes, and it has usually improved the management of a complex incident response effort, such as the one that evolved from the Chalk Point oil leak. Once the structure was applied at Chalk Point, response efforts soon became more efficient and successful. The Safety Board concludes that, because it did not initially put a fully implemented Incident Command System in place, the Unified Command was for several days unable to mobilize and control an effective response to the loss of oil containment that took place on the evening of April 8, 2000.

The Safety Board has previously recognized the benefits an Incident Command System structure may provide during a pipeline spill response effort. As a result of its investigation of the October 1994 pipeline failures on the San Jacinto River near Houston, Texas,[43] the Safety Board determined that implementing the Unified/Incident Command structure and operational principles in the National Response Team's technical assistance document addressing Incident Command System/Unified Command enhances the overall preparedness for responding to oil spills. Consequently, the Safety Board recommended that the National Response Team:

I-96-2

Motivate National Response Team agencies to integrate into their area contingency plans the command and control principles contained in Technical Assistance Document *Incident Command System/Unified Command* and encourage them to train all personnel assigned management responsibilities in those principles.

In a January 17, 2001, response to Safety Recommendation I-96-2, the National Response Team stated that it was working on methods to ensure that all member agencies have integrated into their area contingency plans the principles contained in the Technical

---

[43] National Transportation Safety Board, *Evaluation of Pipeline Failures During Flooding and of Spill Response Actions, San Jacinto River Near Houston, Texas, October 1994*, Pipeline Special Investigation Report NTSB/SIR-96/04 (Washington, DC: NTSB, 1996).

Assistance Document *Incident Command System/Unified Command—Managing Responses to Oil Discharges and Hazardous Substance Releases under the National Contingency Plan*, as requested. The Safety Board classified Safety Recommendation I-96-2 "Open–Acceptable Response," pending notification that the action is complete.

The National Response Team is made up of 16 Federal departments and agencies. The EPA is the permanent Chair of the National Response Team. Since the San Jacinto accident, the EPA has distributed the Technical Assistance Document *Incident Command System/Unified Command—Managing Responses to Oil Discharges and Hazardous Substance Releases under the National Contingency Plan* to all EPA on-scene coordinators, and EPA headquarters has encouraged its regional coordinators to incorporate the guidance from the document in their area contingency plans. Nevertheless, an EPA official stated in an April 24, 2001, postaccident letter to the Safety Board that "EPA currently has no formal policy on the use of Incident Command System/Unified Command." The EPA has not mandated that all its regions use the Incident Command System. Although the EPA's Office of Emergency and Remedial Response is developing an EPA policy position on the Incident Command System, the Safety Board is concerned that no final EPA Incident Command System policy, the development of which began in 1996 in response to lessons learned during the 1994 San Jacinto pipeline accident, has been completed.

The lack of incident command during the Chalk Point emergency response indicates that the EPA needs to make a greater commitment to incorporating Incident Command System principles in its response procedures and to training its people more effectively about the benefits provided by the use of the system. Therefore, to ensure that the necessity of an effective Incident Command System is understood by EPA responders, the Safety Board believes that the EPA should require all its regions to integrate the principles contained in the National Response Team's Technical Assistance Document *Incident Command System/Unified Command—Managing Responses to Oil Discharges and Hazardous Substance Releases under the National Contingency Plan* in their area contingency plans and require the regions to train all personnel who are assigned responsibility to implement the plans according to those principles.

Conclusions

Findings

1. Because Pipetronix incorrectly interpreted the results of its ultrasonic tool data for the pipeline feature at odometer station 53526.55, the Potomac Electric Power Company was not alerted to the need for additional evaluation of the pipe at the location where it subsequently ruptured.

2. Because pipeline operators have no nationally recognized criteria with which to evaluate pipe wrinkles, they may not be effectively determining whether pipe containing wrinkles should be allowed to remain in service.

3. The absence of effective pipeline monitoring procedures and practices, including periodic line balancing, delayed the discovery of the fuel oil shortage on April 7, 2000, which delayed the pipeline shutdown and allowed more oil to leak from the pipeline.

4. Because pipeline owners and operators sometimes do not update their initial reports to the National Response Center, the notifications provided to emergency responders may not always contain the complete and accurate information needed to develop an effective incident response.

5. Because it did not initially put a fully implemented Incident Command System in place, the Unified Command was for several days unable to mobilize and control an effective response to the loss of oil containment that took place on the evening of April 8, 2000.

Probable Cause

The National Transportation Safety Board determines that the probable cause of the April 7, 2000, Piney Point Oil Pipeline accident at the Potomac Electric Power Company's Chalk Point, Maryland, generating station was a fracture in a buckle in the pipe that was undiscovered because the data from an in-line inspection tool were interpreted inaccurately as representing a T-piece. Contributing to the magnitude of the fuel oil release were inadequate operating procedures and practices for monitoring the flow of fuel oil through the pipeline to ensure timely leak detection.

Recommendations

As a result of its investigation, the National Transportation Safety Board makes the following safety recommendations:

To the Research and Special Programs Administration:

Establish quantitative criteria, based on engineering evaluations, for determining whether a wrinkle may be allowed to remain in a pipeline. (P-02-01)

Require pipeline owners and operators to provide follow-up telephone updates to the National Response Center when they discover that the information they initially reported contains significant errors or when they identify significant new information directly related to the reporting criteria. (P-02-02)

To the Environmental Protection Agency:

Require all your regions to integrate the principles contained in the National Response Team's Technical Assistance Document *Incident Command System/Unified Command—Managing Responses to Oil Discharges and Hazardous Substance Releases under the National Contingency Plan* in their area contingency plans and require the regions to train all personnel who are assigned responsibility to implement the plans according to those principles. (P-02-03)

BY THE NATIONAL TRANSPORTATION SAFETY BOARD

MARION C. BLAKEY
Chairman

CAROL J. CARMODY
Vice Chairman

JOHN A. HAMMERSCHMIDT
Member

JOHN J. GOGLIA
Member

GEORGE W. BLACK, JR.
Member

Adopted: July 23, 2002

Appendix A

Investigation

The National Transportation Safety Board was informed on April 8, 2000, by the National Response Center of a fuel oil release from a pipeline that had occurred on April 7, 2000, at Pepco's Chalk Point Generating Station near Aquasco, Maryland. The Safety Board launched an investigative team from Washington, D.C., on April 8, 2000, that comprised operations and emergency response investigators.

No public hearing took place on the accident, and no formal depositions were taken.

Parties to the investigation were Pepco; Support Terminal Services, Inc.; Mirant Piney Point, LLP; and the Office of Pipeline Safety.

Appendix B

Initial Incident Timeline

Day	Time	Events
April 7, 2000	0715	Cleaning pig is launched from Chalk Point Station to Ryceville Station.
	0830-1400	Tank level gauges are taken (but not used to compute line balance) at Chalk Point and Ryceville.
	1430	Chalk Point pump begins cavitating. Meter noise and oil flow stops at Ryceville Station.
	1440-1534	Pepco and ST Services personnel determine that, based on tank level gauge calculations, Ryceville did not receive all oil pumped from Chalk Point. Shortfall of 3,089 barrels is estimated.
	1538	Chalk Point pump is shut down.
	1550	ST Services assistant terminal manager begins trying to report problems to Pepco officials.
	1620	Pepco Chalk Point general supervisor for operations is told of line balance discrepancy of 2,000 to 3,000 barrels and notes shortfall quantity as "2,000 barrels."
	1643	Pepco Chalk Point general supervisor for operations orders flight to locate leak site.
	1802	Report from pipeline patrol plane indicates leak at Swanson Creek.
	1807	Chalk Point emergency plan is put into effect.

Appendix C

Significant Events From Leak Recognition to Loss of Containment

Day	Time	Events
April 7, 2000	1835	Pepco Chalk Point shift supervisor, when pressed, estimates release size at 1,000 to 2,000 gallons.
	1840	ST Services assistant terminal manager confirms in his conversation with Pepco Chalk Point general supervisor for operations that line balance discrepancy is about 3,000 barrels.
	1850	Pepco senior environmental coordinator reports 2,000-gallon release to the National Response Center.
	1850	Pepco spill response teams deploy floating boom in Swanson Creek wetlands area.
	2015	Pepco Chalk Point command center information board indicates spill volume of 3,000 barrels.
	2030-2100	State and Coast Guard responders begin arriving at site.
	2100	Pepco engineering group confirms 3,000-barrel release figure based on tank level calculations.
	2300	Pepco conducts first command post briefing.
April 8, 2000	0250	Coast Guard Federal on-scene representative arrives.
	0330-0530	Coast Guard notifies EPA that incident is in the EPA's geographic jurisdiction and that it will relinquish lead for incident response to EPA Federal On-Scene Coordinator.
	0600	EPA Federal On-Scene Coordinator leaves Philadelphia.
	1015	EPA Federal On-Scene Coordinator arrives at accident site and learns that spill volume is 3,000 barrels.
	1600	Unified Command revises storm plan due to worsening weather forecasts.
	2030	Outer booms at the Patuxent River are breached.

Appendix D

Significant Environmental Response and Clean-up Events

Day	Time	Events
April 9, 2000	Before 0700	Oil plume is seen moving from Swanson Creek across the Patuxent River.
	0745	EPA Federal On-Scene Coordinator contacts the Coast Guard seeking aid in locating marine response resources.
	0800-2000	Pepco contractors attempt to corral the oil plume in the river; they are unsuccessful.
	2100	EPA Federal On-Scene Coordinator orders Pepco to arrange protective booming of threatened creeks.
April 10, 2000	1200	EPA Federal On-Scene Coordinator and Maryland Department of the Environment tell Pepco that the response is not adequate; that the contractors are not being used successfully; and that Pepco's progress reports have not reflected the actual status of the response.
	1430	EPA Federal On-Scene Coordinator asks on-scene Coast Guard personnel to develop an Incident Command System.
	2100	EPA Federal On-Scene Coordinator again orders Pepco to boom the creeks.
April 11, 2000	0300-0715	EPA Federal On-Scene Coordinator again orders Pepco to boom the creeks. Contamination is seen at two creeks.
	1100	Coast Guard representatives arrive on the scene and establish Incident Command System.
	1100-on	Pepco hires contract firm to manage its response. Incident Command System begins to operate. First creek is boomed; booms are pre-staged at four more creeks.
April 12-13, 2000	---	All creeks are boomed. Free oil collection from the Patuxent River is completed.
April 16, 2000	---	Oil collection from creeks is completed.
May 16, 2000	---	Emergency response phase is declared over.